A LOOK AHEAD

Laurance Wieder
A LOOK AHEAD

Selected Poems 1966-2018

Foreword by John Wilson

The roughly chronological selections in this book were chosen from *The Coronet of Tours* (Ithaca House, 1972); *No Harm Done* (Ardis, 1975); *Duke: The Poems as told to Laurance Wieder* (Wiseacre Books, 1990); *The Last Century: Selected Poems* (Picador Australia, 1992); *The Red Sea Haggadah* (Wiseacre Books, 1995); *Ten Torch Songs* (I Saw Johnny Yesterday, 2003); *Laurance Wieder: Greatest Hits 1967-2003* (Pudding House Publications, 2006); *Perek Shirah: A Chapter of Song* (Omerta Publications, 2013); *PoemSite: Songs in the Landscape* (Omerta Publications, 2015); and *After Adam: The Books of Moses* (Highland Books, 2019).

Many poems first appeared in: *Books & Culture*; *Boulevard*; *Buzzi Brueckner*; *Columbia College Today*; *Columbia Review*; *Epoch*; *First Things*; *I Saw Johnny Yesterday*; *Issey Miyake Bodyworks* (Tokyo, 1983); *Just Before Sailing*; *New Observations #43*; *New York Arts Journal*; *Nimbus Broadsides*; *Paris Review*; *Pataphysics*; *Pequod*; *Poetry in Motion #4*; *Scripsi* (Melbourne, Australia); *The Cortland Review*; *The Christian Century*; *The Little Magazine*; *The New Yorker*; *The Stud Duck*; *Trojan Horse*; and on *PoemSite*.

The entirety of "Duke: The Poems as told to..." was also published in *Scripsi*.

"King James Reggae" was featured on public television WNET's *Voices of New York*, and aired by itself as *A New York Minute* on WNET Channel 13 in 1996-97.

Copyright © 2020
Laurance Wieder
Foreword: copyright © 2020
John Wilson
All rights reserved

HIGH
LAND
BOOKS

ISBN: 978-1-7330907-2-8

COVER ART: *Jonicus, the First Astronomer*, unknown artist, *ca.* 1400-1410, The J. Paul Getty Museum
COVER DESIGN: Matthew Morse/ heymatthew.com

CONTENTS

FOREWORD 11

THESE ANEMONES, THEIR SONG 19
    THESE ANEMONES, THEIR SONG 21
    THE END OF AUTUMN 22
    HYMN 23
    THE EXCHANGE 24
    WATER IS THE MOTHER OF ICE 25
    GERTRUDE AND SAMUEL 29
    THREE GENERATIONS AT ONE TABLE ON THE PATIO 32
    THE GOOD LIFE 33
    CLOUDS 34
    HASTENING THUS 35
    THE ROOF 39
    THE WANDERER 41
    AFFECT 46
    HYMN TO CREATION 47

MASS CONFUSIONS AND ENTHUSIASMS 49
    MASS CONFUSIONS AND ENTHUSIASMS 51
    CHORUS 52
    I ATE A MUFFIN AND IT WAS ENOUGH 53
    NO HARM DONE 55
    THE LAST CENTURY 56
    BROWN CATS IN THE DOG DAYS 57
    TWO PRESENTS 60
    SO HIGH, SO LOW 62
    CRUSADE SONG 64
    THE GIANT SUN'S SONG 67
    THIS IS GOD 68
    PROPHYLAXIS 69
    DOUBT SERENE 72

    EMBLEM 74
    ANATOMY 75
    "GOD, SIR." THEN SHE WAS QUIET 78
    JULIA BLOOMFIELD 79
    DEAR ABBY 80
    GNOSIS IN PRAGUE 82
    CURRICULUM VITAE (1978) 83
    CREDULOUS, ALL GOLD 84

WEALTH OF NATIONS 91
    WEALTH OF NATIONS 93
    Body is to spirit 98
    THE MAP OF JAPAN 99
    FINISH UP 102
    SWISS INDEPENDENCE DAY 103
    CALIFORNIA 104
    FOXGLOVE, SOURCE OF DIGITALIS 105
    ART HISTORY 107
    POET, PICK UP THAT GUITAR 108
    KING JAMES REGGAE 110
    FLAGSTONE 112
    YOUR MELODIES 114
    IS THAT ALL? 116
    HAPPINESS IS MY BEAT 118

PILLOW BOOK 119
    PILLOW BOOK 121
    PUNCH AND JUDAISM 122
    VIA SATELLITE 129
    DOWNSTAIRS ON THE GLOBE 131
    GOOFY IN THE MIDDLE 132
    GOOFY'S BRUSH WITH DESPAIR 134
    SONG (FROM THE TAMIL) 136

    GARDEN INTELLIGENCE 137
    INFATUATION 139
    SOME HORSES AND SOME COWS 141
    FAME 142
    BLACK ELK SPEAKS 143

DUKE: THE POEMS 147
    THE SEARCHER 149
    BUFFALO GALS 152
    SHOT DOWN 153
    TARA 154
    KACHINA 156
    THE CLASSICS 157
    BORDERLAND 160
    HELLO, PILGRIM 161
    HARD TO BELIEVE 163
    GRAUMAN'S CHINESE 164
    BIG MEDICINE 165
    SOUNDTRACK 166
    OVERLAND STAGE 168
    THE NEEDFUL 170
    THE LETTER "C" 171
    BLACK HAT, WHITE HAT 173
    AFTERWORD 176

A LOOK AHEAD 179
    A LOOK AHEAD 181
    WHAT HAPPENED TO SEYMOUR 182
    ONE STRATEGY 184
    SIDEREAL 186
    Q&A 190
    SONG IS ANGELS' BREAD 191
    THE DEATH VINE 193

- SERIAL 194
- CARTOONIST! 196
- PACIFIC RIM 197

ROMANTIC 199
- ROMANTIC 201
- CONFEDERATE BREASTWORKS 202
- OPEN AND SHUDDER 203
- FABULOUS, BUT NOT ALOUD 204
- WRITTEN ON THE DAY DEAD GHOSTS ARE FED 206
- A NOTE ON YEATS 207
- SABA'S NURSERY RHYME 208
- GUILTY, WITH AN EXPLANATION 209
- LONG AND SHORT 210
- TODAY 213
- GLIB CONFUCIAN, GARRULOUS LLULLIST 214
- A SOMETIME THING 216
- THE LAST PART OF LONGING 217
- AIR ON THE SIDE OF PRUDENCE 219
- OPUS POSTHUMOUS 221
- SMALL EMOTIONS ARE THE CAPTAINS OF OUR LIVES 222
- HARP 223

COMMON ANCESTOR 225
- COMMON ANCESTOR 227
- WISDOM OF THE GATED COMMUNITY 228
- ORGANIZED DESOLATION 230
- END OF THE MIDDLE CLASS LINE 231
- "WE LOVE THESE MACHINES LIKE WE LOVE
  OUR OWN CHILDREN" 233
- ORIENTALIA 234
- "ONE" IS THE LIGHT THAT SHINES BY DAY 235
- FOUR OLD GERMAN LOVE SONGS 236

    RABBINIC HYMN 237
    SALADIN 238
    UNDERSTOOD 239

PEREK SHIRAH: A CHAPTER OF SONG 241

INDEX OF TITLES AND FIRST LINES 261

FOREWORD

I don't know a lot about Larry Wieder's antecedents, but that's no constraint on the imagination. Perhaps among his ancestors there was a curious figure, maybe a distant cousin of Elijah of Vilna, "The Genius," unmentioned by Martin Buber and other chroniclers of the Hasidic sages: hard to pin down, neither a founder nor a follower of any school.

Certainly in his poetry, Wieder is elusive in just this way. Near the end of this book, in a short poem titled "Orientalia" (one of a set that plays deftly with formal measures), you'll come to a line that demands "Deliver me from solemnity." At which point you'll laugh, because whatever else he need fear, this poet has no worries on that score. And yet if he's never guilty of solemnity, his entire body of work— poetry, prose, combinations of the two, as in *After Adam: The Books of Moses*—violates fashionable prohibitions against worship. A jester is not incapable of praise.

Ruthless with cant (see for example "Black Elk Speaks"), Wieder is nonetheless rarely content with mere demolition-work. In tribute to the sheer excess of Creation, he indulges himself. Nowhere is this more evident than in the sequence titled "Duke: The Poems, as told to Laurance Wieder." The conceit is that these are poems John Wayne composed in his head over the years while waiting between scenes, then recited to Wieder, his scribe. Cutting (and undercutting), the sequence is at once a masterpiece of parody and a tribute. "How did he *think* of that?" So I asked myself when I read these poems for the first time. And yet, once read, the sequence has an air of inevitability! If you haven't read

11

Wieder before, you might start here.

I have many favorites in this collection. One is the short poem "Mass Confusions and Enthusiasms," which begins thus: "Like your psychology, my physics / Aspires to prose out the common magic, / To make something sensible / Of the invisible." Others (among too many to list) include "Doubt Serene," "King James Reggae," "Glib Confucian, Garrulous Llullist," and the concluding sequence, "*Perek Shirah*: A Chapter of Song."

And this book should send you to others—*After Adam*, mentioned above, and *Isaiah's Closing Arguments: A New Translation*, and *Poetry History Music Art: Essays 1996-2017*, all published last year, as well as two earlier books: *The Poets' Book of Psalms: The Complete Psalter as Rendered by Twenty-Five Poets from the Sixteenth to the Twentieth Centuries*, an anthology compiled by Wieder, and *Words to God's Music: A New Book of Psalms*.

In short, a great feast: "In clusters / We press grapes upon you."

—John Wilson

John Wilson edited *Books & Culture* from its first issue (1995) to its last (2016).

A LOOK AHEAD

BEGIN. THE LIGHT IS HONEY.

        Eve stepped from the doorway
Of her purple restaurant
            And said: "Do come.
My special is Valencian
        Paella, made with rabbit—"
I said: "That's against my religion."
She replied: "That's why I asked you in."

                —L.W.

THESE ANEMONES, THEIR SONG

THESE ANEMONES, THEIR SONG
IS MADE UP AS THEY FLOAT ALONG

In 1954, in June
I saw a total eclipse of the sun by the moon.
I saw the flowers fold up, the birds
Stopped singing to the morning, the grass
Grew wet, and it was dark.
I was awake, but when I was awake
A while longer I woke up and said
"I have slept until now," and now
I have stopped sleeping altogether.

THE END OF AUTUMN

From time to time all
the gardens are not the same:
from the gilded to the golden
a slow dissociation:
that's how it's been on my street:
watching the old men creeping up on breath,
the teenagers swimming in the silver wash.

HYMN

The world of the wind is woven warp and woof on the strands of a guitar whose heart lives in the lost cities of foreign scripture fame whose words come from the fire of the female species whose heat warms the words within the cities where harps revise the passage of wind which is the breath of

the cows grazing in the far corner of the common in the northern entrance to the city whose map is carried by the people of the city behind their ribs which feeds the fork where the fire lives which bears the city across the wind weaving warp and woof.

This creation speculation sometimes was a pre-cosmic person whose daughter's baby was his son which broken into fragments became the universe. A goat, he couples with a goat. She is a horse, he becomes a stallion and the world a colt. And so it goes. The creatures of the air the hymns were born from this emitted female. And nothing was missing. And there was no original.

THE EXCHANGE

At first, the sky included the earth.
When the sun and stars came out, the sky
Took the earth and put her in her place.
The earth, separated from the sky, was dumbfounded
And amazed: she wanted to get out of the dark.
At last, the sun climbed up and looked in her face.
And so the earth was firmly established.
And that is where we stand today.

I looked up at the sky and said
Sky, do you have any good ideas?
But the sky answered "Not tonight."
If you talk to the sky it will
Always answer in this way.
Sometimes it answers "Not today."

WATER IS THE MOTHER OF ICE

1

Then love introduces the expensive dream
Of peace into this last report on the future

Of the past, as the pen snaps
Into the gentle discipline.

If it weren't necessary to eat, I wouldn't
And if I didn't have to brace

Myself against fire and ice I would
By all means, relax.

But it's that negligence which leaves the body
Open and the hand gasping for comfort

In the middle of nightmares: certainly
I have lived too long in an atmosphere of hatred.

Discipline propels me through the social superstructure
Insisting "stop and think, pick and choose"

While nothing is satisfied,
Not morning's bleary mirror

Or the later mirror of this afternoon.
This afternoon is colored natural to life.

This afternoon is warranted to neither fade nor spot.
This afternoon is excelled by none in the Union.

It presents the likenesses of children
In from two to four seconds, sitting

And I will not flatter my humble self—
It is a lot better than I am.

Improvements in poetry have not matched
Corresponding improvements in business,

And my life presents an even further halting:

2

What I want compares to the ancients
Who kept records on slabs of stone,

Aiming for a permanence which I
Can only dream of.

Faces flip past like pictures in a book,
Too fast to take a closer look, but

Not fast enough to be ignored.
It doesn't pay to go out for a walk.

It leaves me describing my condition
In leaves or flocks of birds, my feelings

Taking on the aspect of a mountain or river,
Massive, natural, subject to the sun and moon,

Independent of the will. The will
Implies both a future, and a backward glance:

The wishes of the dead are remarkably strong:
They are the breezes of the present life

And buffet the living, like leaves or flocks
Of birds migrating north after a long winter

To cooler regions. And these breezes which intend
To abolish chance create it, and although

The winds can be felt, they too are invisible
As chance, electric, the probable air.

What do I want? I want to leave
Something behind me which is not will,

Which does not challenge the workings of the planets
Or the heart, but includes them, and chance as well

In a breath. Water is the mother of ice
And land of the fish. The sun

Is the mask of evening. Ice, bark of the rivers
And vault of the waves visits in a cold time

And vanishes in a hot season, which equals
The sun. I keep the dull and weekly hours,

Record the natural equations, and decorate
The earth with songs to draw the strings

Of my relations, which tie me to other men,
To the earth, my own body, and the stars.

It is four o'clock in the afternoon.

GERTRUDE AND SAMUEL

Not yet and still was English spoken.
    Der Schmied she sang, an organ
In her chest as well and "O Sam,
    We could be happy."
        If textiles hold firm.
Thence to purchase Tudor oaks
And a sweep of lawn beyond the city.

"Those drapes from Mrs. Whitney's living room."
    The carved elephants from India, in ivory,
The lacquered chest, the Persian rugs,
    A genuine Louis XIV tapestry,
Silk ties, a spinet piano—
    "But all the recordings
Lost in a fire. The whole studio
    Went, you know.

"And I sang for the mayor
    On the radio,
In New York, Paris and Milan
    But the war ended all that
And then Sam wanted me
    To spend my time with the children.
We nine sisters were the toast of old New York.
    All so accomplished. Nellie and Bella and Henrietta

Although they had their children,
    They were jealous, I think, of my success.
But I have tried to be patient
    And do right by them."

"I was the youngest of five children.
    I came here from Hungary when I was twelve
And immediately went to work.
    A Talmudic scholar, my father left the faith.
His wife, my mother
    Soaked our beef in brine.
My ambition, which I almost realized
    Twice, was to make a million dollars.
In '32, I sold out to Dunn and Bradstreet
    And went into imported fabrics."

    At a Bon Voyage party on the *Cristoforo Colombo*
In 1953, my grandfather showed me a hundred-dollar bill.
    I said "That's very big"
Thinking "A lot of money
    In one place." He said
"This is not the first."
    Twelve years later and "Gertrude,
        Bring me the nuts.
That book," he said cracking a walnut
    With a walnut, "is salacious.
Gray's *Elegy*, now that's
    What I call a poem."

"We always liked the good things.
    Sam had his ties custom-made
In England—he always wore a vest:
    We always knew the best people.
We are comfortable now, having led
    A full life, and although it gets
Hard for me to care for Sam (he's always
    So demanding) yet we have
Our children and our grandchildren."

THREE GENERATIONS AT ONE TABLE ON THE PATIO

Their faces weather in the picnic air.
A man lay down upon the ground.
"Between," he said, "the earth and air."
The night diverges on a stair.
The wheel swings around.

Across the bottom of a hill
Old easy Jane and Horny Bill
Fill up an afternoon of chat.
A bentwood cane, a snapbrim hat.
A onetime full and empty chair.

THE GOOD LIFE

Get up at ten o'clock, eat a little breakfast,
    Go down to the sea with a towel.
Take a little sun in a fifty-dollar chair,
    Then take a quick dip in the ocean.
Drink a glass of planter's punch,
    Take a little sail, lunch,
        Ski a little water ski.
Drive home after dinner with three tourist ladies
    And show them the sights with the top down.
Stop off at a bar, drink a nightcap, then
Go home and sleep until breakfast.

CLOUDS

The little tennis ball and the handball blown with wind

Kestrels flagging on the western wind
The heaviness of time could be lightweight

Clouds pinned beneath a paperweight
The sky still perpendicular as I designed it
What beauty

There is no fault at the beginning of a world
Those measurements that don't quite reach the clouds,
 curled
Up or dying suddenly at Pisa on the morning
Of a shoelace, or only swallowed clouds

HASTENING THUS

When I was ten my family went to Europe,
Not with an organized tour group,

But in a Fiat. In Paris, however, we
Took a bus tour, which I remember distinctly:

Our first stop was the Montmartre
And Le Sacre Coeur (one place combining God and art

As was explained in four languages): the white
Cathedral rode a cloud above the mount, in the light

Of that August afternoon. Knowing nothing of absinthe,
I wasn't interested then in tales of bohemian poets and
　　painters who lived a marginal but rich existence in
　　those narrow streets at the turn of the last century,
　　although I might be since.

We stopped next at Notre Dame in the Ile de France
(Until then I thought the Ile was just a boat.) By chance

A Latin service was in progress,
So after taking in the lost art of stained glass,

I left the church interior
And went back to the square,

Which brings me
To the focus of my memory.

Carved figures of the Saints occupy a cleft
In the church facade. Halfway up, to the left

Stands a carving of St. Denis, his head under his arm—
This caused my younger sister some alarm.

An analogy with decapitated chickens was rejected
By us both, as well as several less compelling explanations.
    Unperfected

Visions of the crucifixion haunted my sleep in Italy,
Along with other Catholic imagery,

But, among the urban scenery,
St. Denis' head remains most prominent in my memory.

There also was a Europe without parents:
Riding horseback in Villeneuve, swimming at Clarens,

Riding the funicular between Montreux and Glion
To camp, which overlooked the Chateau de Chillon.

In the castle dungeon I saw the pillar
Where Byron carved his name (I thought he was the prisoner),

And hikes above Glion, the rushing river and the rock
(Rochers des Nayes) where, on a small village green, a clock

Face planted with summer blooms.
There is a corner in the rooms

Of memory, even when the sun stays, dark
And dreadful. There, where two walls intersect the floor,
    a spark

Curves on the joint of three dimensions. Fear
And chaos, monsters from the id, all the crude mater-

ials of life live there, and it was also in late August, on a hike
In the Dents du Midi near the French border, that I saw night

Crash into those red cliffs, and saw (quite literally) the way
Space yawns. That day

We campers went out for a walk on a path
Threading the edge of a 3,000-foot cliff. Half

Of us marched single file toward the bluff that overlooked
    the "Tal."
The other half had turned back to make dinner. While

The sun dropped behind me I wished that I had brought
My camera, thinking "These mountains are as they are
    now once, and sought

For later never will appear as now." But
I had left my camera at the lodge. Thinking like that,

One camper broke into a run, he ran
Downhill along the edge before us calling "Look, look"
    and then

I knew that he would slip.
He hit a wet strip

On the path and toppled forward.
    The mountains swim before a word

Can capture them, and that one shriek
I made then also rises from the corner, high and weak.

Later, back at the lodge, a counselor lost
His watch, which he decided had been stolen. Most

Of the night we sat on wooden benches in the summer chill
Waiting for the thief to confess. No one did. Until

The watch was found next to the Turkish toilet, we stayed
Awake. Since that day I have never played

Too close to the edge
Of any ledge,

Either a New York City
Roof, or rural gorge. I can be, and have been, witty

About annihilation, although it scares me.
And memory, while it halts, never impairs me

While hastening thus,
Minus or plus.

THE ROOF

Here where the jetstreams rise,
The spine of the Continental Divide,
Halfway up a cliff, in air

His hammer keeping time,
His pitons marking climb,
A mountain climber sang this prayer:

> I clamber on the edge of rocks
> The negative of city blocks.
> This granite no god's passive face
>
> This ledge no human dwelling place
> But here the small green lichen grow
> In hollows worn by melting snow
>
> And wind, it hustles through a day
> And blows the fall away.
>
> The bighorn sheep and mountain goats
> Grow old upon these winter slopes.
> Eagles hover in these peaks
>
> No longer signs, as hours and weeks.
> Clouds. The moon emerges from eclipse
> To light the crusted, mossy lips
>
> Of tundra spread below the glacier—
> Snow without erasure.

The rose-hip of late summer,
Harebell, cowslip, columbine,
Strawberry blite, air rarified:

And if the wind rose, I'd lift
And smash my back against the cliff
Or if a cold front catches me

Ascending, I would freeze quickly.
What to possess?

Glacier, crevasse
The drop hard brass—
Listen, the hammer sinks the piton

And it rings.
    My feet on
The short pegs I drive

Keep me alive.
All is mine.

Above the timber line.

This was the prayer the climber sung
While going up the granite cliff.
    His line and hammer gave it lift
And held his body where it hung.

THE WANDERER

Someone wants mercy   for himself alone
The wind's favor   though he's sad
And through sea lanes   long and chilly
Stirs with his hand   the top of the cold sea
The wake of his exile: a man set in motion
The traveler talked   about ships, remembering
The wind's wrath, the war   where his friends fell:
I often sit alone   on the shore at sunrise
And care for what happened: no one alive
Knows what I know   none dare
The sea's clear days: but I know
Great men carry   something large
Inside them, a cloud   tied to the light
And his heart pounds   so he thinks what he can
And stands in that light   the sea wind breaks
Over yes and no   over help and anger
So great men, brilliant   know the heart's dull sound
Is the heart   the line
My mind reels in   from the minded sea
Often troubled   casting off from home
From friends and family   tied to the land
And her children, covered   so I left
Heavily, dragging tackle   a spar on frozen seas
Sought halls and treasure   and givers
Wherever I found   in far or near distance
A friend   some comfort

A party   whoever lives
Knows how poor   a friend sadness is
To someone who   has few friends
The thin exile   not a golden road.

The beaker is chilled   not as earth's glory
He remembers sharing   gold with his friends.
They were younger   were golden
Were singers and eaters   all past, gold, gone
So he who must, knows   his friends
The clear lessons   must go on without
What sorrow and sleep   tie together
That one bound   together alone:
He seems to remember   his father in fortune
May hug him and kiss him,   touch
Hands, knees and head   as once
Years past   he sat in power
That wakes him   man, friendless
To visions before him: the black waves
The gulls bathing   spreading white feathers
Frost under snow falling   mixed with hail
Then the hard parts   the heart holds
Laid open, the pair   born like tears
In the memory   the mind watches
And welcomes   looks over
Its early companions   swimming away
The clouds   do not carry
Words friends are saying—   care recalls

Those who would banish   too often
What waves bind   to the mind.

So I cannot think   of the world
While my mind   doesn't darken
When I think   of man's whole life
How it drops   through the floor
Proud retainers   in this world
Where all days come   to holes and falls.
Therefore a man may grow   wise before leaving
The portions of winter to   worlds waiting, wise
His heart will not heat   tongue will not hasten
War will not weaken   nor foolish
Nor fearful, nor   happy, nor hungry
Nor fast to boast   before he is certain
A man waits   to boast
Until armed and   striking, then he knows
How his heart's thoughts   turn out.
A wise man   sees withered
All this world's   wealth wasted
Flat on the plain   sand on the beach
Where wind sweeps   the walls stand
Frost-covered   snow fences
Fall around halls   falling on rulers
In ruins, the joy   of companions collapsed
By pride   some taken
By battle   some taken
By birds by   the high sea

43

The gray wolf   dealt death to
One, crying, in rock   cave, the man, hid.
Earth wasted   man's mother
Of music and dances   men, robbed of
The old works of giants   stopped, idled:
He then, using wisdom   considers the floor
And the deep   and dark life
In wise clouds   he remembers
Sowing and slaughter   and speaks:

Where did the horses go?   Where are the families?
Where the bright dinners   the presents, the parties?
O the bright cup   the fighter
O power of princes   time passes
Below the dark sail   of night, as if
Never a thread   a shard of the company
A very high wall   painted with serpents
The spears all   ran to us
The arrows were thirsty   for fate
As these stone cliffs   storms break
Snow falling   binds the earth
With white winter   cold tumult as dark
Darkens, the shadow   of night from the north
Drives the hail   in men's faces
All harsh   on the earth
And the course rolls   down under the world
Here property passes   here friends pass the sky
Here man passes   families passing

The floor of the earth   stops her threshing.
So spoke the wise man   he sat alone, thinking
A man is good   who holds to his truth
Nor should he mourn   too readily
Unless he knows   the remedy
To work with his heart   because rest comes
From the sky   to us all
As does mercy   as sure as we stand.

—from the Old English

AFFECT

"It is refulgent," said Rabbi Simeon, "this child,
But he will not grow to be a great man."
"Why?" asked his colleague, lighting a candle.
"Because so much light burns quickly, and at fifteen
He would be too old for a man. The stutterer,
The man with a few answers, endures to old age, and is
The great man among us." The smoke rose
From the candle with his words; vented by the house
    they rose
Above the radio towers, above the twenty-story office buildings,
    they rose
Conveniently beside an eagle, who kept them from falling.

HYMN TO CREATION

Jeremy Bentham, Fichte and God
Descended from a pseudopod.

Aquinas, Augustine, Pico della Mirandola
Didn't compose until out of the stroller

Unlike J. S. Mill and W. A. Mozart
Who practised as infants their chosen art.

William Shakespeare and John Milton
Grew up in England and slept with a quilt on.

Voltaire, Spinoza, Hegel, Rousseau,
Plato, Blake, Byron and Diderot,

Coleridge, Wordsworth, Dante Alighieri,
Rabelais, Jesus, Joseph and Mary:

All of these people and Moses and God
Descended from a pseudopod.

MASS CONFUSIONS AND ENTHUSIASMS

MASS CONFUSIONS AND ENTHUSIASMS

Like your psychology, my physics
Aspires to prose out the common magic,
To make something sensible
Of the invisible. Simple music
Must elude our logic, for the octave
Heard as moving upward through the scales
Registers only as a return, a circle
If graphed, on the oscilloscope.
In that gap between what's measurable
And felt live love and hope—the electricity
That flows about mortality
And charges fact, and makes it what we know.

CHORUS

    Do not begin far from us
    Death is yet near to us
Darkness, and crying, and rust and dismay

    In the small rose, the heart
    Calls the bee to its part
And the bee sucks its pollen, and flies away

I ATE A MUFFIN AND IT WAS ENOUGH

This morning waiting for my ears to clear
I thought about the lucent Milky Way,
Which rotates through the compass through the year

As though it were a cosmic ceiling fan
Churning atomic wind, that is, our time.
This morning, waiting for my ears to clear,
I thought about the lucent Milky Way.

At ten I knew the names of many stars
And thought the names were knowledge.
What to say? The names are far from me.
This morning waiting for my ears to clear
I thought about the lucent Milky Way,
Which rotates through the compass through the year.

Sitting in the dark can be a lark,
Like dancing to no music on a dare,
But in the end, the "it," it catches up

And one might wish one thing had been another,
That one had been less father and more mother.
Sitting in the dark can be a lark.
Like dancing to no music on a dare

The world goes round. At least, I hear no music,
See no spinning. Except their grand effects,
Which nowadays are the domain of science.
Sitting in the dark can be a lark,

Like dancing to no music on a dare.
But in the end, the "it," it catches up.

The greatest crimes are passions undetected
Which twist the great expanse into a knot
That only time may pass through unobstructed.

What does it matter that what passed for beauty
Was awkwardness decked out as a great seeming?
The greatest crimes are passions undetected
Which twist the great expanse into a knot.

The lever wants a fulcrum, life a heart
To see and saw the beam, its up and down:
The too thin sky, the none too solid ground.
The greatest crimes are passions undetected
Which twist the great expanse into a knot
That only time may pass through unobstructed.

NO HARM DONE

The last day of July: the sun is out
And time seems many papers folded over—
Out, in the way a light goes out,
Relentless. But that imputes some sense to light

And time seems many papers folded over.
Perhaps some useful fact will come to light, something
Relentless. But that imputes some sense to light
Which has no sense, and has nothing to indicate.

Perhaps some useful fact will come to light, something
Navigable by the backward sense
Which has no sense, and has nothing to indicate
But, as a great sphere, meets my feet,

Navigable by the backward sense,
Across the smoky lawns and sidewalks of twenty years ago.
But, as a great sphere meets my feet,
The trek is effortless and irresistible.

Across the smoky lawns and sidewalks of twenty years ago,
The last day of July. The sun is out.
(The trek is effortless and irresistible.)
Out in the way a light goes out.

THE LAST CENTURY

The first fall day
In August, clear
The air smells like fallen apples
Around the reservoir
Where gulls sit mewing
On the same tempting blue that lured
The first Emperor of China out
To fish for the carp
Of eternal life.
He fell overboard, caught
Cold, and died.
We, too, are folded
In the chilly leaf,
Are drawn to the destructive moonrise.

BROWN CATS IN THE DOG DAYS

I read a story yesterday:
The fox escapes the hounds
By the strength of his legs,
But the fox doesn't know this,
So he catches his breath
And preens his bushy tail.

"You have been more purely beautiful
Before than you are now," she said.
And I thought: True. October lawns
The leaves held down, and flocks
Of migrants queued in vees, while clouds
Of sparrows eddy in the waveless oaks.
Full of days, the beakers broke in a blue shower
And now, you say, I sit and watch
The little sparks and toss them
Upward, my thoughts the fireflies
Of god, and grown.

In old Russia, an ironworker's father
Studied philosophy very hard, and found
A solution to the Great Question, which answer
He immediately carried to Tolstoy,
Who lived in a hut behind his great house
On the family lands. It was August.
The freed serfs had had enough
Of hoeing and weeding and reaping, and dozed

Below the sheaves, while the Count
Busied himself with his new world.
The philosopher leaned toward Tolstoy's ear.
"Yes," said the Count, "how pleasant it is,
But I do not expect to die." And the sun
Dove into Europe, while wheat waved
To dogs in the wind. Then as now,
The world was almost over.
Brown cats curled by the teapots.
Peaches turned cantaloupe colors in the bowl.

In 1652 a rabbi dreamed
A camel pursued him from one room
To another. Though he locked the doors
With a complicated lock, the camel
Burst through and kept going.
At last the rabbi found himself
In a blue room by the ocean. There
He no longer feared the camel, and
A beautiful woman stepped out of the curtains
And kissed him. The sun set, the moon burned
As the sea came in through the window, and
"From fear and terror I awoke."

But I slept by the sea
Without camels, while a man in a chair
Wrote a brief, and the words "blue chip"
Flew off the page and skipped

South on the ocean, until all
I could see was the sea
And the mirroring sky.
Something is in it
Of the first days, then
Before the oceanic feeling was
The ocean, before streaks were drawn
Like giant airplanes travel, so fast
And high, less useful than disturbing.

Yesterday New York was clutched by a cloud
That swallowed all the scrannel noises
And turned the streets starling with blotches
Of brown, and the dusty accordion
Player who thinks of himself
As the Ancient of Days
Cursed a few quarter-tossers
In a language known only
To his accordion.
                At times, the great beyond
Hangs fire, and everyone
Catches a breath, and it seems
Like something really will happen.
It does, of course, but not
So gaudy as thought. A quiet
Change, as an angel
Moving a wing through a century,
Waiting to be called.

TWO PRESENTS

The parrot Mephistopheles learned to call the cat
When he lived in the kitchen, and later mastered
"Cracker" and "Hello." The falcon in his yellow eye
Dilated at grapes, peeled carrots, but blanked at the sunflower
Seeds he shelled in his foot. Five years of this
Until my father bought the bird a mate, Irvina,
His green double, even to the orange fringe
Above her beak. They fell in love, and after
A week-long courtship in the summer cage, they shared
One perch, a happy pair of half-moon parrots.
Although they made no egg, they called to the migrant
Birds that lit on the kitchen window. One December
Irvina died. Mephistopheles withdrew
To a corner of the cage and watched her carried off
In the business section of *The New York Times*.
A cloud of listlessness descended. He would not bite
A finger, but rather plucked at the pale
Green feathers on his breast continually, become
At last a naked, mournful devil. Removed
From view, the parrot lived another seven years
But never grew his feathers back, and would not talk,
And could not fly, as covered in a sheet
He whistled like an oriole, until.

The door swings on its hinges, a fly's wing
Without will or explanation. Walking down
57th Street, below the race of the adoring

Clouds, I don't feel connected to the crowds
And their concrete business, although I am.
Spacious, I remember Solomon Ibn Gabirol,
Born in Malaga, at an early age discovered
He had remarkable gifts. One generation
After his star set, it was written:
"None ever did his station reach;
He above his generation towered."

SO HIGH, SO LOW

"I am remember the time, in Italy
Where Girolamo took my friend aside
(He couldn't say this to my face) he said
'Jimmy, he used to be a good radical
But America spoil him, he is not
Like me.' What the hell. Forty,
Fifty years ago we all think, all
But me, 'The Communist,' but
Kropotkin, he say then, and I agree
That if the Communist keep going
(This was 1921) the way they go
In twenty year the world will come
To hate the name of Russia.

"But maybe I have changed, and maybe
None of us be what we think we are:
We want the money, we take it easy,
We get fat and grow the hair.
The children don't think how we do,
They don't want the dollar, but
They call themselves the radical. Pfui.
They call names at the police.
In Italy the priest and the policeman
Would kill you, and nobody waste his time
With names. One time when I work
On the ships (I just come to America)
I meet a friend, a anarchist, and he

Want me to run the whiskey with him
Because we fight together against
The Communist. 'You must be crazy,'
I said. 'You do this and you only find the trouble,
And what is your life then?'
                Henrietta, now
She's stopped the work, we both
Have time to go to opera. We watch
The television on the Watergate, but any country
That give you only two choice for the election
What can you expect? No difference
Between the one man and the other.
All of them make the people to hate
The name of government. Only the anarchist
Is any good. Only the anarchist, and I
Say this after more than seventy years living
And I always say this, like the Prince
Kropotkin say in 1921."

CRUSADE SONG

These feats of earth shall bring us to the air.
The past caught fright like colds
And old guitars hymn our libidos
Which guide us with Orlando and his birdbrain
Legions on to Bethlehem. The broad plain falls
Away from the Glum Mountains. Are we Turks
Or Huns or Tatars that we hang before the sack
With camels passing? Equals must remain
The same, even in the green and mortal eye
Our company berates the old administration
Who draw their bathrobes off beside the Jordan.

Leave us not grow torpid peccaries back home.
Our death is not so dear as what we know.
Nothing has been done anyway, for troubadours
To sing into a lady's hearth.
Remember history! Remember Scipio Africanus
And Alexander! Save your rice for bread
And can the marriage rites! There is a gauze
That overlies what shall be done, and your grandsons
Will look back to now with pleasure, thinking
Then, then men were men, there was revenge,
Adventure, and no foes besmirched the almanacs.

God leases out his salve. Our wounds will heal
With our hiccups, and the fright will pass
And we will rest, andirons, each with his fellow

And the fond boats will lie along the pillars
Rising and falling in the fans that turn the tides.
We shall be martyrs to the winds, the very winds that nightly
Crown the pines and meadows of our dear Provence.
At that fair house no churl dare to complain,
And the shepherd calls the Caliph's grandson, his retainer
To carry out the slops, or fan the forge
Which heats the blade that made the Moslem melancholy.

Our song sounds like the edges of the neap tide,
Our companions dressed like falcons poised to swoop,
Our marks the iron mountain and the lion,
We come like flames from Flanders to the flat grainfields here
And fire our French-forged lances at the spaces
Turk dogs dare to fill. Grr. A red and sober hour.
They'll wish they'd slept with cobras in their camp
Or straggled at the Bosporus and drowned
Rather than face the terrors of our conquest,
A face more terrible than twenty sieges without water in
    the Sudan
And the troops of Cæsar lurking at the gate.

Draw a pot for the collector of uproar.
Beware, o snake, beware the mailed heel.
Death, do not think to eat our company—
It's not your fate: we're all going
To Paradise, in style, like Elijah.
The passive mares of passage clear our way.

French horses, raised within the moated fastness
Nose their enemies aside with evening oats
And grazing as they go, 'til not one blade remains
Below the heavy bells around their necks
And death shall no more visit them, than shall the phoenix
Fly into the sun again, with all our company.

—*after* **Raimbaut de Vaqueiras**

THE GIANT SUN'S SONG

Who turned over in light
On the sky's soft floor,
The size of a leaf
That moved us so,
As Elizabeth's finger
Stirs the guitar strings.

Fateless, like the sleeping
Newborn, the sky breathes.
A cloud blooms, appoints
The buds and nodding
Always, touches what seems
The milk drunk stars.
They reel, always.

Yet it's given to us
Never to move from the spot.
Light dwindles, it falls
On pained men exchanging
The hours for hours
At a clip, as water
Dashed down the lip, long
Years into uncertainty.

THIS IS GOD

This is God as an ageing Jewish man.
Note the moustache and the fringe of hair.
He has made some good investments
And is pretty well fixed,
But he has sorrows, too.
It's the sorrows made him
An ageing Jewish man.

PROPHYLAXIS

"It must have been exciting,
Having your father for a father:
He was always edgy, looking for adventure.
I remember once he came to see me
At the office. We discovered
Both of us had plans to spend that weekend
In the Catskills, and he said:
'Let's get together.' That Saturday
We sat around the table having lunch—
Some other couple and your mother—
And your father said:
'I think I'll buy a car.'
That afternoon he went down
Into town and bought a car:
That must have been three thousand dollars,
And he didn't even know the dealer.

"Why, my father used to take me
Around town with him, it could have been
Him walking a dog instead of me
For all that happened. I suppose it stuck.
Even when I was a teenager, horsing around
With my friends, and we would see
Who could make up some crazy stunt
For us to pull,
I couldn't think up even one. Not ever.
Know who I respect? Composers.

Writers start with something, have some model,
But composers pluck the sound out of thin air.

"There's an expression, it's called
'Stop the World, I Want to Get Off.'
Well, that title really got to me.
I used to lead my life
Looking to other people to give me
Direction, never thinking that it might not be
Necessary to pursue the almighty dollar,
To do this or say that, and I became
—Don't think I mean too much by this—
A little odd, a bit out of the mainstream
And I have kept clear of business
Ever since. It puts a different slant
On things. You know,
There just might be a story in this,
The story of a man a little different,
Reflecting on the everyday, life's foibles.

"Have you had an X-ray lately?
Certain of my patients have developed
Cavities I've somehow overlooked
While probing with the instruments.
True, it's not good to overradiate,
Yet it's possible to go too far
The other way. You have discomfort?
No? Then let's wait

Six more months. I know that money's
Short, and you'll be wanting it
For other things.
You may rinse now."

DOUBT SERENE

The author of *The Incoherence of the Incoherence*
Must have recognized the stars' influence
On his prevailing fiction, though he probably
Didn't see diseases like influenza or anxiety
As symptoms of the lust for order, making
Metaphors of metaphor and mathematics into mastery

Of the soupy real by contemplative space. Mastery,
Then, like negatives of newsreels, makes of incoherence
An unrecorded counter-feeling which tries to influence
Those difficulties taken in the sun, probably
Succeeding only when the stars tick and anxiety
Rises, haze between the heavy trees and heaven, unmaking

All that stellar certainty which was of one's own making.
Bare a white flank to the host of blankness, blanket mastery
Over both the half-remembered childhood spent in
    coherence
And scientific play, which has a half-uncovered influence
On what is done today—constellations of behavior probably
Are our astrology. But no prediction comes without anxiety,

Flux doesn't make me feel as snowmen do for flakes.
    Against anxiety—
The thought one hasn't got it right—is making
Do with the materials at hand, repeating maybe mistakes
    maybe mastery

Of those who take the body for a map of incoherence
Framed by ice-glazed trees, that doesn't influence
The course it courses. Probably

All is as it should be, but I don't see it—probably
Some defect in my faculties. Or is the method answering anxiety
Different from the one that lets green hang in the air, from mythmaking
And bookkeeping and getting and letting and betting? Mastery
Then beams with native clearness, a lens through which the incoherence
Shines like a silver fish of uncertain size, flashing in fluence.

Down that transparence streams the bodied shadow of the influence
Other pasts refer to the stars, or caring gods, improbably
Personal, but just as clearly addressed to the common anxiety
To get it right for once. Here is darkness in the making.
Not to be afraid of it is all the mastery
I wish for, not to warp the darling incoherence.

For incoherence is the mother of all mastery,
Making whatever hope and happy influence
Bathes us. As anxiety's the freezing of disorder, probably.

EMBLEM

A shadow box where Pierrot
Strums a guitar and serenades
His femme, his fool, his fantasy—
The moon is full, it pulls the strings,
Unwinds the works of *Claire de lune*,
Of dangled engines of a dance
Done in despite, in means and moans—
Small chips of light, of heart, of sound.
All sparkles in the air, and clatters down.

ANATOMY

"'You talk in rhyme, it always sounds
Like rhyme,' she said, and I replied
'It sounds like rhyme because it's right.'"
"You can use that," Chuck observed.
"There was this problem, then, between us—
The intelligence…" He stroked his goatee
Once then trilled his fingers in the air.
"And she had little secrets. Like her name.
We lived together for three months before
She told me that her name was not the one
She went by at the go-go bar.
I told you how we met? A friend
And I went to this topless bar in Queens
Where, between the pinball
And beer mugs banging in the bar sink,
By strobe light, I saw her
Flash G-string and pasties, Queen
Of Sodom, as it were, wreathed in her power.
I exaggerate. Anyway, she stepped down
For her break. We got to talking.
I had never known someone like her
(Her mind I mean), so when my friend
Said he was leaving for the City,
I took a chance, and stayed.
She got off work at 4 a.m. She had a car.
When I suggested she could drive me home,

She looked me in the eye and said,
'You could be a pervert.' I said,
'You could, too, and I'm not worried
About me.' Anyway,
We drove back to Manhattan and sat talking
Parked near the entrance to my building
Until one in the afternoon.
Next time, she came upstairs.
We lived together for three years."

He sipped his brandy. "The thing between us
Got more difficult, showed up
In funny ways. Like giving presents.
Once, a month before my birthday,
We went to the Francis Bacon show
At the Metropolitan. It made her nervous—
Didn't stay long—but I said
Before we left that if she ever
Wanted to give me a gift, I'd like
The catalogue. The morning of my birthday
She went out for several hours, came back
With a package, put it in the closet,
Left for work. I knew what was going on,
Said nothing for two weeks, then took
The book down from the shelf. She said,
'O yeah, happy birthday.' I said, 'Thanks.'
We fought a lot. She didn't wash. We fell apart.

"Some months after we split up
A lady friend of hers and mine said
They had come by my apartment
When I wasn't in, and Wren
Had gone inside and stayed there
For an hour. But everything was
In its place, so I filed the incident,
Figuring its meaning would become apparent.

"One year later I was cleaning up
Before I moved my stuff up to the country
When, behind the radiator in the living room,
I found a note—that
Accounted for the hour.
It said (I will not quote):
'I was here, but you were not.
I wanted to tell you you were good
For me, to touch you once more just
To say goodbye.' I put that note
Into a painting, to show her
She was part of me, but the one time
We met, by chance, she spat in my face.

"That was, I guess, my last romantic love.
I'm over forty, not so crazy anymore,
And think I will go back to teenage girls."
"Some story, no?" Chuck said,
And we three talked at length
About the power naked women have.

"GOD, SIR." THEN SHE WAS QUIET

Love answers
Fear. The drink
In the basin.
Come closer, the lens
Of the lowering sky.
Come closer. The breeze
Softly shakes
Down the dogwood, the wall
Of azaleas.
A grief and a pleasure.
The bee and the rose.

JULIA BLOOMFIELD: 24 JUNE 1974

Days are skirts, and years the wind that raises them.
Who sees the white ankles time shows, praises them.
Time is the great parter
Of the waves, of people straining for the garter.

That's an airy conceit,
But Julia is steady on her feet,
Tending the garden
Days, so they don't harden.

Watching flowers, she becomes them,
Slightly tongue-tied (in dreams all's not said)
And even if she sums them
Up, they're only flowers in a flower bed.

Time is the great collector. It's brought
Us together for a birthday, no more serious
Than anything else that's been remarked, or thought.
As life gets older, life gets more mysterious.

DEAR ABBY

Dear Abby:
    I have met a boy,
A sculptor with a fine blonde crew cut,
Orphaned, versed in mathematics, winner
Of a statewide science fair at seventeen
Who understands my inner nature.
Once, I kept strict orthodox
And rose each midnight to address
My prayers to God in his chosen tongue,
Shunned pork, and stayed clear of my wife
When she was bleeding. That was easy. Lord,
Who am I? Who are other people to me?
Can we be fathers and be fair?
These doubts tormented me.
They drove me out of business
Into art, which is no place for little boys.
Can he be faithful? Or do men who love men always
Kiss and tell? My wife will take me back,
But I don't want to wrestle with my nature
For a lifetime. Is it true we die
And nothing gets left over, neither spouts
Of ecstasy nor bitter flakes?
If so, then what's the point?
I have bought the boy his own apartment,
One with northern light. Should I
Pay the utilities, or should he

Take some responsibility
Which would teach him to grow up,
The value of a dollar,
And just how much I really mean
To him?
    —Rapt in Manhattan

Rapt:
    It's better if you make him pay
The monthly maintenance.
You take the mortgage, which can be
A tax deduction. Ask your wife
What else she needs to keep her comfortable
For rest assured, there is no better peace
Than a household in good order.
You are your own best judge.

GNOSIS IN PRAGUE

The painter took a slice of air
And called it his own—
A black square on a black field
With a whisper of light behind.
The door is ajar.
                      At dusk
The sun turns red, say the Greeks,
With a blush as it enters the bed of dawn.
In fact the falling sun turns red
Because it is falling apart
And the dark earth rolls out to catch it.

CURRICULUM VITAE (1978)

Byron reborn as a suburban Jew,
Wordsworth after analysis,
Blake with glasses,
Keats recovered,
Shelley knowing how to swim,
Marvell on asphalt,
Donne but just begun, Ben
Jonson thin without Latin,
Hölderlin with a taste for Chinese,
Rilke with a part-time job,
Mallarmé in English,
Pindar of the aesthetes,
Horace farmless,
Dante stuck at home, and
    committed to short works.

CREDULOUS, ALL GOLD

An almost real speculation—parts
Will keep, parts
Drop. The lake in flood
O'erleaps, or rather, o'erlaps
Its banks, a full coffee cup
On a wobbly table.
    Full of O's, mushrooms on October
Lawns, and how the leaves seem
Placed, as if on purpose.
          As if?
Cried the oriole. As if.

Harder to remove than a cranberry
Stain, it occurs
"That one thing, unsayable
But assumed—the self, perhaps
In its most reduced, elusive sense,
An initial, remains
Unwritable—allows one to think God's name
Unpronounceable, and god in man."

Speech, too, is a kind of wickerwork
Woven about the sense and feel
Of things, the spirit's cage.
"Drop the bars, let it go, poor thing"—
But when that small bird escapes

As it will, who could tame it
Though it call out its name from afar?

Sparrows flock over a ballfield,
Staying on for the continent of winter
As the mother of all changes her clothes.
There is a time to huddle
Under hills indifferent to the wind
That tears them down, and a time to be drawn
Upward to an early bed.
Something is hanging in a tree: the thought
"Upon a leaf" and other gems
Of the external soul,
The rag a little person carries,
His talisman against the folds of darkness.

"Our sunrise in childhood is a candle in old age."
"Your gorgeous language, guilt and restitution."
The arras flaps. The wall is bare and cold.
"Decide. Are you a looker or a taker?"
"This napkin from Prince Henry's Portugal."
I was there twice. They sold boats
Beaten out of gold and chased with silver
In the airport shop. The sun just risen,
The tarmac spackled by a sunrise squall.
But coming back the boy slept on through Lisbon,
And so farewell that westward with thy streams…

The child dreaded the day the sun would grow cold
And wondered what life was for, then,
And what people would do. Before
Came that beginning, that happened long ago.
And draws back, the way a wave curls back
To show the bottom, or the bottom of the wave.

Beyond the city limits, beyond
In fact the city of the mind with its own
Crowd- and cloud-capped towers, surges, electricity,
Stands a vacant plain, where one
Is just the size one is, and distance
Brings forth things without comparison.
No shadows there, unless one hold a light up.
No darkness there, unless one's eyes are closed.
All still. Such starry music. Windy tremors.
A pebble's been displaced.
The worm labors in darkness.

Measure, measure, measure, measure,
Measure out the days.
Card the cat and marry the canary.
Mop the floor.
Turn out the lights.
Fold the lofty linen up.
Our lives are rock.
The clear days water.
The air a thought.
A breath the border.

Measure, measure
Years brought by on trays.

Very soon I shall enter bitterness.
Very soon the sights will turn to windiness.
And soon the street,
    the low grade's gentleness
Descends the omnibus
That cometh after us.

Raft on a row of air.
We stay. The sun goes by.
Stars later. You and I
Are better when such things
Inside us glare. Pillows.
Sheets that slake.
The earth a bed.
The air a lake
For a time calm smooth.
By the time we notice
They stay, we move.

At night the covers close
Sweet face, so you need look no more.
No more upon the cashmere days,
On clouds that ride the veil shoulders,
On Demeter crushing beetles, sowing grain,
On windows stained with ivy,
Windfall, landfall, footfalls in the hallway

And no one before or behind.
A horse stomps in the emerald blast.
The shadows fall in colors,
Themselves degrees of darkness,
As Helios rings for his whetstone,
As a man taps his gold-tipped umbrella.

I know how I want it to end.
As it began, in silence
And the drift of a large impatience.
As though, arms down, refusing
To fly one could transcend
Not the arrangement
But the distance between bare trees
Beckoning the pomegranate sun
To mount yet lower in its solemn space
And that transmitted firmament
That when I speak up turns
To cream swirls, smoke in a teacup.

The dead fold their umbrellas
And call for the gods, who remain
Beyond the hollow sprinkling crumbs
Of light on shades afflicted
With a rapture of the shallows.
Shallow as a building in a puddle,
Shallow as Sarmatians sweeping over,
Shallow as the arch of an eyebrow,

Shallow as the full moon in a bare sky,
In a watercolor of Korean moonlight.
There, too, snow falls into the colorist's water,
A tern paused in imagined flight.

WEALTH OF NATIONS

WEALTH OF NATIONS

"Economics, Andrea, my love
Is like psychoanalysis: a science
Of the darkly understood. Look—"
(Pointing to the frog-voiced vagrant
Seated on the sidewalk who sells
Ball-point pens to passersby on Second
Avenue)—"a depressed man doing
Depressed business in a depressed time.
With insight into self or spending money
He might be there—" (pointing
To that radiant wedge, the Citicorp tower,
Just then chiselling a low cloud)—
"Or maybe not."
                We wandered on.
"Consider. Money is completely human.
No god invented ready credit; no god
Or priest can gloss the whole economy.
It goes its own way, rises, waffles, bolts
Down Wall Street, a tide with its own rules
Like the unconscious. You have heard the story
Of the three philosophers engaged
In a dark room to explicate the elephant,
An animal they'd never seen? One grasped
The trunk, and said, 'An elephant's a hose
Venting moist air.' The second, underneath
Its stomach, said, 'The beast's a hairy leather

Canopy.' The third demurred: 'We have
Here pillars crudely formed, and creaky.'
Prolific metaphoric bulls and bears,
Street humors, panic, overconfidence
And current numbers for the navigator
Dot maps of that uncharted sea,
Stretched at the edges, the economy.
But on these figments real ills attend:
Hunger, idleness, despair.
Yet like the deep neurotic bound to his
Compulsive round, the patient can be helped
Through insight, healthy vigor of the mind."

    "Oh, come on," Andrea said, as we stepped over
A derelict's crossed legs while he slept
On a cardboard mat over the exhaust
Grate of a Park Avenue bank,
"This talk will never keep us from the poorhouse,
As my mother used to say. Or," skirting
An unscooped poodle poop, "from starving
Like dogs in the gutter."

    I laughed.
"Fears. Family fears." Crosstown traffic essayed
Gridlock. "America's no place for nervous
Nellyism. Look in this shoestore window.
For ninety dollars you can buy
A pair of sneakers that perform the same
Work as a pair available for seven ninety-five

At any upper Broadway discount shop.
But the ninety-dollar pair is more efficient,
An investment in our children's future
Way of life."
    "I thought we had to save
To send them to good schools," my loving chuck
Replied.
    "The thought's naive, if not subversive.
Industrial societies
    Thrive on efficiency.
        Efficient production,
            Efficient consumption:
                Each begets the other.
That's the beauty of the high-priced sneaker:
One thing for the price of ten.
Why pay less when you can pay more?"
We passed a drugstore dressing up
Its windows for the Christmas rush.
"As Jesus said, you lose your soul
To find it. And the meek inherit. Paradox,
But central to our being
Here. That's Marx's failure:
He saw contradictions bringing down
The superstructure around our bourgeois ears.
In fact, they are the wit, the dash, the *verité*,
The glue. Glum Karl Marx
No better comprehends this Christmas shopping

Than—" (we passed a bank that offered
Cut-glass bottles filled with gumballs
To new depositors, plus high-cost loans)
"Than disco banking."
                The sidewalk on Fifth
Avenue was blocked. Two three-card monte
Dealers and an arab hawking "Bullwhips,
Six dollars, genuine leather," drew a crowd
Of get-rich-quick suckers and seekers
After the odd bargain. "Poor sheep, chasing
Chimeras when they could be spending, making
More to earn. If only…"
                "Nyah," snarled
A short man wearing chains, "why not go back
Where you came from." And the crowd turned ugly.
    "That will do," my love said, hauling me away.
"It's bad enough you haven't got a job.
I don't need you dismembered."
    "Hold on. I work,"
I said, stung. "No one pays me, true,
But with no money come no money problems.
My mind is clear, my spirit's up.
Remember when I went in to an office
Every day: no windows, headaches, arbitrary
Orders, lunch, fluorescent lights and styes?"
    "Yes, darling, but not all the out-of-work
Have your resilience. Some kill themselves. Some others.

What about them?"
"I don't know.
Perhaps you're right. When I was younger
I believed that every human being
Had some gift, some gleaming, only buried
By dull teachers, honking politicians,
Television and the yellow press.
If they could find, could treasure up that spark…"
　　"… they'd perish like dogs on the road to the poorhouse,"
Dear Andrea observed.
　　"Unemployment."
I shuddered, thinking of more lines.
"The great blot on our name as reasonable,
Feeling, social creatures. But perhaps
The new technology, say, cryogenics—
We could freeze the unemployed until
Their services are needed, or until
Someone discovers what to do with them."
　　Andrea giggled, "Do you think there's a chance
We'll finally get snowbound this winter?"
A west wind stretched out all the flags
At the United Nations. Nearly home.
　　"Good evening, sir." The doorman leaned
Against the door and handed me a package
From an undecided publisher.
And messages were on the phone machine.

Body is to spirit
As cloth is to body
Grown to its own size:
Room in the air.
Air in the weave.
Waves in the breeze.
The earth spins and
Things come to an end.
So, day and night,
A body blooms
At its own hour.
Stretch the pause
Through the sky,
Or float–muted banner–
Signs, no designs.

Signs, no designs.
Or float–muted banner–
Through the sky,
Stretch the pause
At its own hour.
A body blooms
So, day and night,
Things come to an end.
The earth spins and
Waves in the breeze.
Air in the weave.
Room in the air.
Grown to its own size:
As cloth is to body
Body is to spirit.

THE MAP OF JAPAN

"We're just a couple nearly forty
With a baby and no money
In the bank. This isn't Larchmont."
And this isn't parchment.

This isn't parchment, yet it's paper
Largely floats our modest venture.
Debt's a caper to our credit, both
In earnest and a figure with no matter.

So, guilt hedges the security. No matter what,
The last fall trees turn colors from the top
Down, in three strata—archæology
Of the unexcavated future, yours and mine.

It isn't yours, it isn't mine, save
For the moment. Chinese characters
Blocked by the sun on red brick walls stir
Up a calligraphic, watercolored feeling

In another tongue than this, which puns
On the great whoosh, the crack, the sweeping
Backwash of a creeping race. Asleep,
Or half-asleep, I watched the bamboo

Shadows of imperfect glass, the shutters
And the trees outside play on the nursery wall
Cast by the passing headlights, and I thought
No thought except the sight, as painters

Might if painters with an oriental bent
Had kept my bottle vigil
In the watches of the night, and all
Their difficulties were just mental.

If all my difficulties were just mental,
Would they be on the wall map of Japan?
The watchword among nations Hiroshima,
The cresting wave, the bullet train,

Love suicides, a broken spray of pear, all
Spare and untranslated? Teenagers are elated
By art and music, which will never die, at least
No more than we do, shaking dice and humming

"Merrily we roll…" "Row, row…" by rote, on faith.
Before the last malignant habit's turned
To smoke. Hooray. Just knuckle
Down to work today. Eat something. Practice

Pirouettes, tune up your instrument
And make it good, or new, or what you will.
If not, then worship as the city
Pigeons do, in wheeling flocks

Above the towered altars of the clouds.
No heaviness allowed, no tense or gory
Spectacles— just retell a modest story
Brushed by the coatsleeves of the crowd.

FINISH UP

A leaf, when torn, becomes
An instrument the wind plays
Airs on, no repeats
But in bits, where no one
Movement says it all, and
What's vocalized vanishes,
Leaving what fits.

Animal, vegetable, mineral:
A botany student recorded his dream:
    I sat at a table, wondering
    What is it?
    Where is my ego?
—a feeling most uncomfortable.
Animal, vegetable, mineral.

SWISS INDEPENDENCE DAY

At sunset, the campers take
Their shingle boats down to the lake
And, lighting candles, let them drift
Out toward the middle. Weak as stars left
In the city, their liquid pin lights
Snake and gutter, wax and white.
Little did the homesick boy
Suspect a time would come when
He would feel homesick for then,
Or that the tapered fleet that Alpine night
Would feel more permanent than clay
Dogs modelled by his daughter,
Than teenage love and what came after,
Than the bathtub at his feet.
How nice to soak and rhyme a quarter hour
Away in a hot shower:
The morning sun makes rainbows in the spray.
To win the lottery you have to play.
Between the steamy billows and the solid
Porcelain's our world, *The Book of Pillows*,
Where "Man is Free" as ornamental
Pear trees shaken slightly by the wind.
They demonstrate the trunk and root
Are real, and though the foot
May catch, the dancer fall, the lake
Swamp the candles, it's no mistake.

CALIFORNIA

One afternoon in the lounge of the Gem Institute
A young woman in short skirt and high boots
Sat near me with a cup of coffee.
I said to her: Don't get upset.
It's nothing that I can't control,
But I confess I have
                          a mild foot fetish.
And she replied: Shall I put my feet in your lap?
    Oh, yes.
              And she did.
Later I overheard her talking to her girlfriends.
It was the most exciting thing to happen to her
Since she came to California.

            Read to me,
Young lady, read to me this passage from *Justine*.
I've closed the office door,
The principal's away at a convention,
And I trust there's little stronger than the bond
Between a junior high school teacher and his student.

FOXGLOVE, SOURCE OF DIGITALIS

"I know an old woman
Who sleeps with a hammer.
She worked all her life
As a waitress, and saved
Until now she has jewels,
Owns a condo in Florida,
Put her one boy through medical school.
The son has a good practice
In obstetrics, in New York, but he
Betrayed her: he married
A woman. The old mother
Keeps their wedding portrait
In her pocketbook, and shows it
Every chance she gets, saying:
'See that woman smiling?
Why shouldn't she smile?
She married a doctor.'
And raps the chair arm with her bangle bracelets.
Which brings us to the hammer.
The waitress had a premonition
She would die in the night
Of a heart condition.
At bedtime she lays out her diamonds
And pearls on the nighttable.
With her last gasp she plans
To smash all her jewelry

So she can die knowing
Her son's wife won't wear it.

"I love to quote poetry
As I make the grand round
And after, at the daily
Mortality session. You know,
Not an intern could tell me
The name of the poet
I quote—(he wrote
'Do not go gentle into that…')"

ART HISTORY

I said to the psychiatrist:
> I feel depressed.

He said:
> You've left your wife,
> You're living in a dump,
> Your dog is dying.
> If you didn't feel depressed
> You would be crazy.

I remember one large fight we had,
Pearl smashing glass and tearing
All my work down from the walls.
She shook a sketch pad underneath
My nose and screamed:
> Paper, paper, paper, paper,
> Everything you do you turn to paper.

And she had a point.

POET, PICK UP THAT GUITAR

A friend whose name translates as "honorable"
Told me about a couple he stayed with
Outside of Boston:
                Dan, the husband, played
Around with other women and his wife,
Barbara, stood for it, to keep intact
The family unit for son Josh.
Dan had his own true love in New York City
Named Barbara (ruling out
A possible confusion), and always came home
For breakfast, every morning.

Aside: Dan was compulsive. He collected
Every book he came across
Written by a "Dan." He said:
"I have a thing about my name."
His father's name was Dan.

One evening Barbara, Dan and Josh ate dinner
At Dan's parents' and stayed over.
After the families retired, Dan
And his mother stayed up drinking vodka
In the living room. His mother, out
Of nowhere, started telling Dan how she
Felt horny and could not decide
Whether to use her hand or go down
To the corner bar and hustle up

A one-night stand. Dan blanched.
His mother said: "Enough of me.
How is your marriage? Things look strained."
Dan droned about his Barbaras and breakfasts.
His mother struck her head and groaned:
"I should have told you. All my friends
Who knew said I should tell you."
               "Tell what?"
"Years ago I had a brief affair
With another man. That man's your father,
Dan, not Dan, and now the pattern reappears
And you will wreck your marriage."
"You don't know. I never told you. Mother,
Josh, I'm not his father."

Navigating through the fog,
The melodrama, many captains
Use an aid: triangulation.
It would appear less neat, less dangerous
To cast this tale in prose, as fiction,
But nothing fits together half so well
In fantasy as in imagination.
That's why the floor
Supports us, why
It thwarts.

KING JAMES REGGAE

The mixed multitude kills time in Kingston airport.
Outbound flight delayed by bus wreck on the road.
    The last paper on the newsstand
    Sports a white girl's naked breasts.
A tropical depression's turned the Trade Wind to the east.

Our short hop across the island passed through turbulence.
All week the downing of the innocents shook heads:
    The Gulf is an abyss:
        How many dead? Whose fault? Who swears?
A question thumbs its *Holy Bible* in the heat.

What is one man to do faced with such wickedness?
Such wickedness as lies cannot conceal?
It had been twenty years beneath blue white red yellow stars
Since ball lightning pulsed while turtles climbed the beach.

The two-lane coastal highway reeked of cedar.
Hempfires whispered to the full moon,
    Fields of dancers chugged to train songs,
And old dreads departed swaying heads
    Marked batswings in the air.
Even now the Sunday radios hosanna.

Human nature is one nation in the darkness.
There a bearded man stepped toward me in the shack light.
He peered into my face:
    "Do you believe in the Most High?"
I could answer:
    "Something larger and outside me."

Shops do business. Children fidget on hot benches.
Older transients form a long queue at the bar.
Some change dollars; some write postcards; most
Just watch the airport monitors for word
When they'll be leaving where we are.

FLAGSTONE

1

Walking past an iris
Yesterday I thought:
My eye is in love
With this iris, but
How can we live this way?

2

Folding the Hudson's Bay
Blanket that cushions
    The seat of the prickly rattan,
My daughter said: "A half," and
"Daddy, if we eat, we will not die."

3

Better even than the scent of camellias,
Than the dense cloud of night-blooming jasmine,
Than the tea air of roses, the rock of wisteria,
Is the smell of fresh cash. Himalayan spring.
Able to have everything; able to need nothing.

4

Though I knew from the start
There was no living in it,
    I chose poetry.
    Though I knew
There is no love without
Parting, I chose you.

5
>   That night a highway
>   Crew came in a cherry-picker
>   Crane and changed the dead
>   Bulb in the streetlamp to one
>   The color of moonlight.

6
>   At the National Academy,
>   The Buddhists all wore business suits
>   And mixed their orange juice with sparkling water.
>   >   At the Botanic Garden, bees
>   Try overpowering a flaming peace rose.

7
>   And I do remember yesterday,
>   >   How you waited patiently
>   To music that they danced to in the old days:
>   >   Three crows sitting on a maple limb
>   >   Drive the starving strays away.

YOUR MELODIES

God is so angry with us
That he takes our wits before
He takes our life. This candle,
Guttering, should last about as long
As my supply of music paper, always low,
And my pen runs slower than the melodies
Spill out. My father reckoned I could teach
The alphabet and figures for a living, anything
Else I wanted to depend upon my salary.
That's how the world goes. On the other hand
I hear the praise of a deaf master, and every
Second thought loops in that measure
Bridegrooms dip to, into laughter
Dapping like a troutline on the working waters.
And then I'm out of time,
Don't even know if I am wearing glasses.
The songs make what's inside of things
Come out, the table legs wear dancing shoes,
And millstones grind in matrimony slowly,
But exceeding fine. I have to have
My little puns. They trouble
Neither God nor the convictions of the choir.
I need to walk along the avenue
And drink in like a mannikin the fables
Played before shop windows, listen to the gypsies
Hawk their versions of a future gleaming

In the ball of chesty hope and murky fate.
I must go out, I say, but some pain
Pins me to this chair, and keeps me
From out there, as though the scene
Were but superfluous attachments
For a rare machine. But when I go,
Perhaps to eat a meal, down
A glass of beer, and meet and greet
Those friends I still see frequently,
And even those who crop up after many years
At a funeral or wedding, after shaking
Hands and wishing well, I taste
The ashes of a former flame, the tremor of old slights.
And I'm at my wits' end.
And don't know what it means.

IS THAT ALL?

"Six month ago I was a rich man
And I don't know it: I have
Freedom, money, house, the family....
Today, that's all gone crack. Today
Is Easter and the Passover.
Do you believe in God? I say
It all depend on what you mean.
If you mean God is someone I
Must love so he look out for me
Then I say 'No, I don't believe.'
From when I was a little boy
Of nine year old at dinner with
The mother and the father—in Trieste
Where people kneel to the Pope—
I know there is no God.
       Church
Is okay to meet the girl
To marry, like a club, but I think
Jesus was no real man, you understand,
Because at that time Jewish people
Marry young, boys at fifteen,
But Jesus never marry. Who he hire
To work with him? The fisherman.
In Trieste everybody know
Nobody stupider than fisherman.
Today nine year ago I go
Into the hospital for operation.

That time I think, 'I'm dead.
Seventy-six.' But no, today
Is I stand here, and Henrietta
Is the one.
          When I come to
This country, in five month I speak
The English better than I do now
After sixty year. What the hell.
Is not important no one understand me.
You know, I could do anything,
Go visit Europe if it was
Just me alone. Like yesterday
Was beautiful, I want to fish—
All time I love the fishing—
But no more. Instead I sit
Beside the bed, three in the morning
If she call.
          Look, Peter come.
Peter, you are the half and half,
Half Christian and half Jew.
Is lucky, you can take your pick.
To me the holiday is just like Christmas
To the child who don't believe
In Santa Claus: he don't expect
But maybe he still want the present."

HAPPINESS IS MY BEAT

My head aches, my right arm twinges, my stomach gripes and roils—
I will close my eyes just for a moment
I will take off my glasses and nap for an hour
I will curl up and sleep until morning
I will stay in bed for a day, for the week, for a month, until spring, until autumn
I will not get up again
I will close my eyes and lie down forever

PILLOW BOOK

PILLOW BOOK

Mild but wild, April day with winds
That make tall wavers of the cedars.
Peach buds wearing lipstick blow
Pink blooms. The Japanese dwarf plum,

"Abundance," lags. "Daddy, what is doom?"
Too many pillows give me a stiff neck.
To be famous in my lifetime
On another planet. On my own

I watched a seagull perch atop
A reed-bound piling, but damned
If I could sort the fruits by color
Or by number, or could match

The right word to its picture.
A tipped-in map, "The Holy Land," marks
The Twelve Tribes of Israel—(not
The edition with Christ's words

Spoken on earth shown in red ink.)
The picket fence repels all stranger dogs.
I could have answered, "Girl,
Forget the hags," as the nature

Of her question begs, but words died
On my lips, which threw kisses
In their pithy place, of monuments
Now pencilled in the landscape.

PUNCH AND JUDAISM

Years pass like days, days
    Feel like years. At four,
My daughter beat the steamer pot
    With dowels, 'til the knoll
Grew Himalayan. Her Tibetan drum.
    October. Panicked crickets
Scattered where the rake tore up
    Dry thatch. The south face
Of that maple yellowed. Before,
    I turned my bicycle to watch
A purple mallow nodding in the cattails.
    Before that, I cut switches
From a willow just to whip the air.
    That was the time I wanted to be old;
Wanted to be tall, and to find wisdom.
    Last night the moon rose higher
Than the sun, the ground mum as pines
    Threw down their needles.
My daughter told me: "Daddy,
    We will die together. Do not worry.
I am very old." A muffler coughed.
    I struck a match,
And let her light the candles. One
    By one, the zeros dream:
One god; no true religion.

Ring, ring: "This is the Center,
    The center of Shadow
And Life?" Wrong number. Ring:
    "We have you booked
For your departure. Check or charge?"
    The sycamore's
Bare branches craze the empty cup,
    A china glaze that spills
My upturned gaze back to the saucer
    Earth, which stretches
Truth, and southward to the water.
    "Daddy, sing. Your lullaby's
Too short. Please make it longer.
    Make it plain, an easy
Plan so I can understand.
    I want to fill
My cowboy boots with mistletoes;
    My soles will kiss the walk."
We rolled big snow balls in a ring
    To make a fort.
We made a man. The wind kicked up.
    The sun grew weak, day
Gray with white tatters hung high
    In the air, white
On gray, like a gull in a gale.

"America's been ruined by
    The coffee break.
There's no need to be rich,
    Just to get by
In comfort. I thought I'd work
    Until I dropped,
But an old blockage in my heart
    Has acted up,
So goodbye, independence. The bills
    Are snow, the money
Water. Better get a job. You know,
    My father never said one word
To me 'til after I was twenty. He
    Was angry at my mother.
My first wife was a creature of her habits
    And those habits got
The best of her. I wanted to paint
    Pictures for stories, not
Build houses, but my brother ran the family
    Business down, so I did
What I knew. Daughters are not sons.
    When a date came to the house
To pick one up, I'd meet him at the door
    And ask, 'Whose little boy
Are you?' Worked like a charm."

～

The jays and cats are not amused.
    "At forty, you will have
No friends." Not true. "You've other
    Fish to fry." "Your own
Worst enemy." "You make a ghastly
    First impression."
"Money's drawn to money." Maybe.
    "You'll be dead
Before you're understood." Not that.
    "You grasp at straws."
"You're dreaming." "Fool." "A dish
    That I no longer eat."

～

    "I ought to give up
Parties," the survivor violinned,
    "Nothing happens
Once you're past the door." That shuts
    Its ear, that breezes
Past my shoulder, beams at others, snorts,
    Withholds the love
The mother's child thought would never
    Sever, humble psalter
In a litany of numbers. "Sledding covers
    Many motions, such as
Lying in the snow, and rolling over."

~

"Have you got a minute? Do you mind
    If I (don't mean to pry)
Ask you a question about politics?
    Understand that in the 'sixties
I had long hair, too, smoked dope
    And walked through India.
When I was there I thought about a lot
    Of things, and since, I've started
Wondering, What if? What if, to take
    Just one example, revolutions
Going on right now in South America
    Were not just civil wars
But military actions funded by our enemies,
    The Russians, say, to weaken us
Just like the Right said they were doing all along?
    Suppose, to take it one step further,
That people for disarmament (and I
    Don't like nuclear war any more
Than you do), and those people are sincere,
    Suppose that nonetheless the Communists
Take full advantage of our system, which permits
    These idealists' dissent, and make
It serve their own agenda which is, say,
    World domination.
What would you say to that?"

My daughter named nine planets out
    Of order from today's
Dim sun, and shivered after every one.
    "There are two earths—
The one that's dirt, and then the world."
    For her, the cartoon
Characters lived long ago,
    In history,
Like Pilgrims and the presidents.
    One starry night
She pointed to the bears, and asked
    "Where is the milky part?"
A man approaching seventy who gave up
    Smoking after fifty years,
Cut back martinis, upped donations
    To the temple, and devoted
His remaining days to tending assets,
    Doctoring his will, said:
"I felt better after all my teeth were pulled."
    Or so the stars
Sang in my own cartoon, with death-
    Defying gravity
And solemn Solomon.

~

Because all the slow singers had died,
    We walked through
The dry snowfall. Evergreens
    Groaned in frozen
Daylight as the son and father
    Nodded, chatted
As if time had not yet passed
    Behind the hedges
Of their frosted picture. "Don't
    Let on that I
Was here," the older man repeated
    Through the taxi
Window. The car pulled into traffic
    And was not.
That's us, who know we do not know.
    The black cat, hunting
For a warm spot, played tom-toms
    On the door screen.
Serpents' new year, by the moon.
    My daughter said,
"The slow singers are all dead.
    The fast ones are
Alive. But one. Do you believe
    That song is true?"
I don't, but I like it, so I sing it.

VIA SATELLITE

The moon waxed fat
From right to left,
A lawyer peeling
Off his suit
Of darkness. Commuters
Nodded on the rails.
I cracked the atlas
Open to a happy page
Where sand bars shrug
Tan shoulders, making
Surf. Judging only
By the map, the earth's
Grown older.
    "The bill's
Right here." The dog
Was forced to wait
Outside. A hazard,
Braking on wet leaves.
"Can you hold?"
    "Can I
Get back to you?"
    "I want
To be a bank next Halloween."
Return to the *Titanic*, sinking
Rates, the evening meal, the sun
Setting below a shelf of purple

Clouds drenched with light
So potent that it cast no shadow
On tenements turned monuments.
One bears a sign: "Third Rail"
Painted lightning.
    "Can you bring
Two flashlights to the Tropics?
A percolator and appointment
Book? Wait. If I'm late,
It's a flat tire."
    October,
Each day fairer than
The next, and colder.
    O suburb
Of the sun,
    O ocean, way
Beyond the bars that keep
The near bay calm, shine,
Gently scour the horizon
Of the autumn wader,
Of the winter clammer.

DOWNSTAIRS ON THE GLOBE

Three weeks of cold
And Patchogue Bay froze
Over from the sandspit clear
To Fire Island. Mornings,
Gulls hop where once
They dove, and mew, and turn
Their noddy heads to follow
Baymen trudging 'cross the plate
Who stop, chop fishing holes,
Blow on their hands, drop lines,
And wait. The bay
Gleams black, pink, gun-metal, not
The fly's-eye mirror usual
But fixed, now, as the casual
Pickup driver parks on the pier
And aims his headlights south
Across the ice.

GOOFY IN THE MIDDLE

The phone rang late last night:
It was Mickey, wanting to sing me
Some song he'd just found about flowers.
I always try to stay up for the sports
Report and weather. It's hard
To make it through the news. Just think,
I could have run for President, or maybe
For Vice President, but Donald told me
That the best man wins, and Mickey
Never went for speechifying.
Babies sure are cute. Trouble is,
Since Mickey hypnotized me
Into thinking I was the Phantom Blot
And my unconscious mind led us
Straight to The Blot, my eyes close
By themselves, and I forget what happens next.
Mickey said, "Let me sing this
Before I lose it." It was a story
About Minnie and some morning glories
On her trellis Pluto used to sniff
Until some bees got mad and stung his nose.
One time I shook some salt on a bird's tail.
The bird flew off. An eagle. Maybe
If a Mexican guitar band strummed
The carioca and some señoritas danced
Before the first commercial, or I ate

Milk and cookies, I could stay awake.
But every time I go to dreamland
Earlier. Sure is lucky
Mickey called. I might have slept
All night in that big easy chair
With television on.

GOOFY'S BRUSH WITH DESPAIR

I went out and bought myself
A new suit off the rack—
For a long time I'd been hoping
The right girl would come along—
But when I got back home
I looked in the mirror
And began to cry, and changed
Into my old clothes again.
I'm more comfortable looking
At where I've been than where I'm going.
As it says in this here book,
There's no way of telling whether
Other life exists beyond the stars.
It's mighty dark tonight.
I wouldn't sleep well knowing
Someone's staring down on me
From outer space. In fact,
I don't sleep well not knowing.
Last time I fell asleep I dreamed
That agents of a foreign power
Headed by Black Pete, had chained
Mickey and Minnie to a rock
And rolled it off a cliff
Into the ocean. Only I
Could save them, but I stared
Like I was hypnotized

And didn't care. I don't think
I could have saved them anyway.
At least I could have tried.
I'd better drink some lemonade.

SONG (FROM THE TAMIL)

A man may earn millions,
Dine with guests at fine restaurants,
Own cars, boats and houses,
Keep numerous mistresses,
Yet if he lacks children
Who toddle on carpets,
Who stretch out their small hands,
Throw food on the floor,
Smear the baseboards with paint,
Chew their fingers, their books,
And laugh as they step in
Their soft chocolate ice cream,
Then all of his days as a rich man
Are nothing.

GARDEN INTELLIGENCE

1

    A stone bench in the cotton shadows.
    First dew on the lawn, then dust. Someone is walking.
    The heaviness the heaviness of clouds.
    O cover us, and now and then disperse.
    The bumble bee humming, "Alas, how the thought
    Drowned in overflowing," and hovers.
    The way a tulip falls apart, or a rose
    Opens, or an anemone, to death—eternity
    Looks like a rose, larger than a stadium,
    With light where the bees would go.

2

    And sing a song, a song I sing
    Under the Tuba tree.
    Whole Saturdays of sad pianos.
    Of rowboats in the rain.
    Blear mists, deep horns, light pocket sounds,
    An echo of this or that.
    And the dance, I dance
    The elephant reel on rubber legs
    To the cold coffee cup, to the melon, the stair,
    To the cookie of contemplation.

3
    Strawflowers, ornamental grass and other everlastings,
    Honesty, Job's tears, sweet William, statice or sea lavender.
    Time's longer than the time of butterflies.
    The monarch floats below the blue umbrella.

    A monarch floats below the blue
    Umbrella in the time of butterflies.
    The redwing blackbird in the reeds
    And other everlastings: a particle,
    An ornament, like stars and what the thunder meant
    With dark where the bees would go.

INFATUATION

Just thinking about being
Dead at my age gives me
A headache: there was poker

With Ted gulping dope and drink
Roaring: "Two aces, fuck a pig's butt"
(I don't think he was bluffing)

And, by report, by my age
All his teeth fell out, he only got
Up from bed (off the couch)

For a dump, or an interview, a shot
Of whatever. Then he was not.
On the other hand, I wrote a letter

To a dying friend this June as though
He were already dead. I took
Advantage of his foreknown doom

To say things left unsaid in the five years
Since last we spoke. Told him
I loved him, cursed the joke

His body'd played on him, on us, and closed
With him ever in my thoughts at Passover
And other turns God takes. Why bother

When there are no grapes to gather?
Why gape at clusters dewed from the refrigerator?
The swag lamp ticks. The ceiling fan on low.

A big hand for the little fellow, grappling
The ghost of his not-dead father.
I dreamed about him Friday night,

Walking barefoot through the cotton shade
In shorts, a toddler dawdling behind…
The child peered into a coconut husk

Tossed against the wall of conch shells
A few steps from the beach. No way to reach
Whatever web he'd spun inside the hut,
To know if he was lying in the bed he'd made.

I woke up without the headache
Of an unremembered dream, and vowed
Aloud I'd write a letter. Forty now,

I may know better. But the barometer
Has sunk below complaint, while the heat—
Archtypical July—has stopped

The fluted edges of what's owed.

SOME HORSES AND SOME COWS

A bow tie, a green bow tie with sparkles:
Tuck it under my chin like a violin.
Stop crayoning that singing salamander.

The cloud in my mouth tastes like yogurt.
Let me look at the moose on your beer.
I have no cup. I can't say "Cheers."

Help! there's an ant on my socks, and
Roar! the lion has made a design, but
Don't be afraid, it's a friendly lion.

What a relief. Is that the whole moon
In the sky? Bye-bye, I'm going to Bombay
To see some horses and some cows, and sleep all day.

Blow out the candle in the pumpkin, bumpkin.
No kissing on my cheek, just kissing
On my back. I said, no kissing

On my back, just kissing on my knees.
Not both knees, only kissing
One by one. No talking. And no looking.

FAME

Dinosaurs died with meat on their bones
Dinosaurs died with meat on their bones
With their feet in the mud
              they turned into stones
Except for the ones that grew feathers

BLACK ELK SPEAKS

The only state I've never been in is Alaska.

When it comes to restaurants, I'm not an adventurous kind of guy. I don't take potluck when it comes to food.

What? No potatoes?

You know me. I'm not a diplomat.

Never eat a hamburger in a restaurant: you don't know what you're eating.

The best watch in the world is the IWC. Patek Phillipe is also a good watch.

You should have gone with me to get that. (or) You should have told me what you wanted to do. I could have gotten you a better deal.

A yellow diamond is worth more than a white diamond.

Live and be well, your mother will never have to worry about her security again. If I should die tomorrow.

Don't worry, you're not gonna get stiffed. I just want to park it myself.

There's a very good delicatessen in Los Angeles.

That landlord, if I had to do business with him, I'd watch out for the fillings in my back teeth.

Contractors will rob you blind.

You know what's wrong with America? The unions and the blacks.

I went to my attorney's office just the other day, and he put me in the way of what may turn out to be…a real sweet deal.

I should have word on that definitely by Thursday.

This could prove very advantageous to us all.

What we do for your sister, we will do for you.

You know mother and me, whatever we do, it's no strings attached.

I don't want to sound negative, but I always try to think of the worst thing that could happen. That's only realistic.

Every time mother and I have made a plan ahead of time in the last ten years, something has happened, and we had to cancel. Sometimes we get away on the spur of the moment.

I've had it every way you can imagine: standing up, sitting down, standing on my head. But let me tell you, I didn't know what happiness was until I met your mother.

Mother didn't sleep a wink last night.

Did you phone this morning? There were three calls on the machine, and they all hung up.

A Tanqueray martini, extra dry.

I gave him a little lesson in business.

If this is sirloin, you can kiss my ass in Macy's window.

I used to have a real thick head of hair, and I was as thin as a rail.

...The next thing I knew was, I woke up in the hospital.

I would never drive a small car.

The leather on these shoes is just like butter.

Cashmere falls apart.

You should know better than to try and sell me a suit because of the label.

I've been dealing with this jeweler since 1958.

We just kept churning our money.

The more affluent the apartment building, the colder the people are. Until it goes co-op.

Your sister has made a few mistakes. She's stubborn and won't listen to us. But she knows she can always come to mother and me for help. Just so she learns from her mistakes. That's all a person can ask.

I couldn't be prouder of you if you were my own son.

They want the impossible? I give them the impossible. But they have to pay for it.

The rest is gravy.

DUKE: THE POEMS
as told to Laurance Wieder

THE SEARCHER

Any man who'd burn his draft card
Will also burn his bra. Those birds
Who squawk loudest about justice
Haven't got the sand to stand up
When the chips are down. I remember
One time I was mounting this new filly
For the first time when the phone rang.
Heavy breather. "Well,"
Says I, "well pal, if you can breathe
So hard, why not come by
For a breathing contest. Hardest wins."
Then she whinnied. Wham! His handset
Slammed back on the hook faster
Than jack rabbit with a greyhound
Bearing down. That filly. Yes.
You know, I feel about horses
The way cowboys are supposed to
About women. Take Marlene Dietrich:
Maybe she was born a kraut, but she
Spoke the international language
Like a native, if you take my drift.
Lots of times, when John Ford had me
Sitting on some horse's back
Take after take, until I couldn't tell
Which end hurt more and my spine
Would start to cave in, I'd just picture

Her in garters with a chair
Back between her knees, and mine
Would straighten up. Look,
I'm not going to lie to you, not even
If you ask me about Santa Claus,
Because somebody's got to tell it plain
And, with the stuff the newspapers
Serve up and people swallow, what
Does it matter if I tell the truth?

You've got to think a man's outsides
Are what he's made of. If we had to
Climb inside a fellow's head
To know him—like spelunkers,
Little lanterns on our hard hats, bumping
Into sweaty rock and bat shit, sitting
On stalagmites, echoing, flickering, lost
While overhead the sun dried wash
Hung on lines, and red leaves piled
Underneath October oaks—
We'd be gophers. So we go
With the hand we draw, and pay
Only when the other guy has more
To show. Almost Indian poker. Sometimes
You have to spank a kid for his
Own good, not because you want to.
Principles can make a person hateful.
That dope who burns his flag may think

He's saying something about freedom,
But he's only saying "No" to someone
Else's truth. You can't play the game
And cry about the rules. Too many
Good men died without a sniffle,
Put aside their little doubts of right or wrong,
Left their wives and families for
Some European ditch, some jungle mine,
Some six inches of Pacific beach.

The sea is calm at Malibu today,
A low cloud sits on Catalina. Far
To the west, waves break
On coral shallows. Is it death
Or sunshine that's the cheat?
A person could take now to Doomsday
Chewing on these questions, and never
Find he's any closer to the answer
Than when he started, none the wiser.

BUFFALO GALS

Hello there, little lady.
That dress looks mighty pretty
On you, not the gingham
But that way you fill it.
Care to walk with me a way?

Thought I'd stroll out
'til the moon rose
Over Copper Canyon
And the desert turned
A shiny frying pan

Where we could sizzle
In cactus shadows, coyotes
Startled by the cries
We'll raise, puffing dust clouds
In their snooping eyes.

No offense, ma'am, meant
Or taken, just forget
The invitation, just
Forget you ever had
A chance to yodel, to dance.

SHOT DOWN

I didn't want to act the goof
For our guys who took the Sugar Loaf
On Okinawa. I knew the boots
And hat and spurs were out
Of place in front of that Hawaiian curtain,
On that stage, and so I passed
My hand before my face.
An actor, too, has got to go
Where he is sent, just like a soldier;
When your president tells you
What to do, you do it,
No matter if they clap, or boo.

TARA

Sunrise in the High Sierra,
First light dents the summer glacier.
A timber wolf slinks off. Elk browse
The bottom land. Dew beads webs
The spiders spin between scotch pines.
Here a man can scout the mountain
Lion from a distance, and feel how
God must, witnessing what people
Do. Shut up in a bottle, in a jam
Of cars, why not just eat the barrel
Of a gun, and get it over?
I'm not much for fancy thinking, but I think
A man's been given brains for something
More than sniffing his way from dish
To dish, from drink to drink. I think
This world is like a moving picture
Of each of us, for each of us to watch,
And get caught up in. Sure, it's sad
Sometimes, some days so tense
It hurts to look, yet who could tear
His eyes away, could bear to duck out
Even for refreshments? A lone harmonica,
The chase, an old guitar plucked string
By string, until the moon goes down.
At heart, I'm just another tramp
Along the rails, loafing 'til

The fast freight. Some call the whistle
Time, some take a chilly fright,
Some answer with their own low sound.
If there's a God, involuntary noises
Which escape like steam through fissures
Are the prayers he hears.
Not my gravel voice, or yours.
Marked one by one, awake
Or dreaming at our post, against
That bar we hardly measure up.
Give me a shot. A double.

KACHINA

The hidden grows. Those chants and steps,
The magic circles the old shaman drew
Inside the tent of skins, the doll
He waved to snatch near dangers clear
Of the sick soul, I never found
The time to learn or understand much
Less believe in. I treasure simple things
That are not me, that come from far away
And talk about what I can't say. I can't say
Why, but it's my nature, like Yosemite.

THE CLASSICS

Spend over half a century
In the motion picture business
And you're bound to wonder
About truth and power.

It's okay to confuse me
With the parts I play,
The real hair on the toupee,
I'm acting myself anyway.

But parts of my own life
Frankly stump me, hint some
Invisible director, backstage
Voices, forms behind the kliegs.

As a schoolboy I loved Latin.
Gaul is divided in three parts.
My given name is Marion.
My real initials are three M's.

Each of my three wives was Latin
American. Would a mystic say
That I was born to play the Latin
Lover? the marrying kind?

I walked a long time in the shadow
Of the tall man in the Stetson,
A man who paints his face and feels
Valuable, who sees himself as little

As possible. I can tear myself
Away from the mirror, easily.
Drink leaning back against the bar.
Hustle through the powder room.

Better to stand like a lodgepole pine
In Monument Valley, than have to turn
The knob and find a crowd of strangers
In my closet. When I'm called upstairs,

I don't want my friends to read the Bible,
Raise a stone. Just burn
My body. Throw the ashes overboard.
If the spirit lives on after

I'll be looking down, although I've got
A snowball's chance in hell of anybody
Honoring my final wishes. Long speeches,
Sobbing women, the last coffin nail.

Words work where action fails.
I never talked or acted cheap, as corpse
Or one-line cameo centurion.
What got me on this, anyway?

The shock at seventy of seeing
Me alive on-screen at thirty-three?
The sea swell?
This damn heat?

Saddle up.
Nobody's perfect.
Not everybody's
Tried so hard to prove it.

BORDERLAND

To the south, a cloudburst
Slicks the peaks, here
Heat lightning flickers

I'd be the ground
Your toes tap time on
The ear of corn you grind

Your folk song

Play the basin
I'll become the Amazon
Snake for ages down

Our course, your delta
Lazing in the rushes
I can take the heat

HELLO, PILGRIM

A little man might have to get
A little drunk to speak his mind.
A big man might have to get
A whole lot more than drunk
To figure out just where he left
His boots. I didn't want my kids
To hear me yelling at my second wife,
But I'm not about to feel sorry
For what's happened. When I call
A fellow "Pilgrim," it's because
He hasn't reached El Capitan,
Because he's got the trail written
On his face. Tibetan lamas pray
By spinning wheels. So if a fellow's
Always got his wheels turning,
Even if he doesn't get around
To outright praying, he may have
All the religion he will need.
Calling to the man upstairs
Is like lecturing your kids:
The more you say, the less they hear.
I'd rather work. I'd work even if
It didn't make me rich as Croesus.
It makes as much sense as a mountain
Does to someone in the valley.
On the Atlantic, winter waves

Look like mountains would
If they were weak, and we could
Move them, with talk.

HARD TO BELIEVE

Waking up each morning
With a million dollars in the bank
Feels good, no argument.
Lose the getting up,
A hundred million doesn't mean much.

Bull elephants, fatigued
By battle and their memories,
Turn solitary rogues,
Then stagger, heaped-up tusk and bone.

Hard to imagine twilight porch light jumping checkers,
Big city home game on the radio.
It's easier to play tall in the saddle.
It's easier not knowing where I'm going.

Forget the doubles. When I can't shoot
My own stunts, wash off the war paint.
Leave the part that's like tobacco
Smoke, like liquor in a dry man's brain
Who's stopped believing in strong medicine.

GRAUMAN'S CHINESE

Sid, there are no words
For what it feels like to stand
In cowboy boots, in wet

Cement. Instead, I drove
My fist into this sidewalk
Where the stars forever set.

BIG MEDICINE

This poor excuse for a singing cowboy
Never shied away from a woman
In war paint, or a showdown, or a hoedown.
It makes no sense to play some weepy
Painter at the tulip party scared
By what he sees, when you're strong
And ugly. It helps to show some manners.
Six-feet-plus in stocking feet, I couldn't hide
Behind a skirt or what went on inside of me.
That's why I sit down like a veteran
Apache war chief smoking packaged cigarettes
While young bucks whoop around the fire.
No Indian could ever dance like Fred Astaire.
I never found, or lost, my Ginger either.

Sometimes staring at the ceiling on a late night
Turning in, the mattress rocks a bit, as though
The big machine had stalled. I try to keep
In motion, so I don't have to listen to the lies
My body tells me, but when I drift I hear
The wind out back blow hard, and boulders
Sag like paper bags. Time was I might have lost
My temper. Now a good day's one that I get out
Of bed, and there I am, and didn't make it up.

SOUNDTRACK

My music was the crack
Of jaw against a fist,
The splintered straight
Back chair against a bar,
The craze left by a shot
Glass pitched into a mirror.
Like I said to the drygoods
Merchant fingering his wares,
"Tuck it away. If I were you,
I'd save that thing for bait."
The trick was timing swing,
Impact and camera angle
So that wince and grunt rang
True. My third wife strummed
Guitar and sang the sad songs
Of the south 'til I forgot
The Alamo, the foreign enemy,
Myself. And who's to say
That I was wrong? A man
Who kicks a man named for a dog?

Once I outgrew my puppy fat,
I worked because I knew
The horse, the rope, the business
End of a repeater, hopes
And what came after better
Than I knew my kids, or how

I knew they were my kids.
When a puppy whines, you either
Let him howl, or let him in,
And what you make of him
He stays. No new developments.
No self improvement. In love,
As in the movies when the rain
Blows hard across old pasture land,
Watch out. Zeros at twelve o'clock.
Apache arrows. Talking drums.
The Padre shouting, "Cheer, boys,
Cheer like Protestants," and me
With little faith at all,
And that a sign of weakness.

OVERLAND STAGE

Don't think back much
To early times
When shooting dimes
Off tree stumps pleased
The girls, especially Louise.

Colt forty-fives
At fifty paces,
My partner's dummy's
Wooden face,
Those little touches would impress

A corn fed Kansas
Toast of Europe
Pair of brim full
Champagne glasses.
Just tall, and strong, my name not yet

Mythology,
In hero's getup:
White sombrero,
Pancake makeup,
Real hair and teeth, an opera

Cowboy actor.
When the lead sings
Tenderfeet dance
For the ladies.
Gentlemen, the dust we eat.

THE NEEDFUL

It's lonely off the reservation,
Bad flats and white man's water, but better
Riding out at sunup to a showdown with my nature
Than waiting for somebody else to finish
Washing, so I can go after.

Too many years spent playing just
Myself left no time over to be husband,
Father, anybody else except a man who walks
By falling forward, upright, with no net—
One who's had to catch himself

Talking about things I might not
Know, unless I stopped midstream, looked
Past the bank, the moving train, the summer snow caps
Before I said the rest of what I had
To say, if I had to say it.

THE LETTER "C"

An easy way to take off weight,
But it's tough to sit up straight.
Doc said, "Good thing
You never were a dancer."
Didn't have to ask why,
Didn't need the answer.
I taught a clumsy boy
To dance with bayonets.
I held my women easy.
How many get to waste away
Aboard a yacht in company,
Can pay a little lady not a nurse
To fetch the dose
And read the mail?
Talking doesn't help
Make going easier,
    Just longer.

For half the chances of a Chinaman
I'd fall for everything again:
Lights, smoke, the gullies
Liquor makes on ice. Politely
Smile at the joke, how
Living right, the beast
Gets tamer. Look her in the eye,
And name the time and place.
Some things it doesn't pay

To know.
    "*Sí, sí.*"
For one:
    your Alamo.

BLACK HAT, WHITE HAT

Marlene didn't like it when I rode
Out of town any better than
The others did. I liked her smell. I told her
I would wear her garter on my sleeve
Until somebody came along
Strong enough to take it off, but she cursed
Me like a gambler down to his last dollar
Damns the greenhorn raking in
His stake. Soon town was swallowed by the dust
My horse kicked up. Near fifty miles of sulfur
Flats and alkali before a well,
The trail marked by cattle skulls, by wagons
Capsized, broken wheels, by bumpy ruts.
I loosed the cinch and walked. A condor shadow
Slid across the desert like a clear creek
Over stones. I could make the water hole
By moonlight, once the snakes and lizards fed
And crawled back underneath their rocks. Coyotes
Howl. No Comanche here. No white
Men neither. A twisted oak, dead long before
Conquistadors dreamed Eldorado lay
Over the horizon, marked the spot.
I spread out my bedroll, hobbled dobbin,
Smoked a cigarette, turned in. The moon
Set. Her throaty words came back:

"No human tie
Will hold you, scout
The sea of faces,
Prairie grasses,
Old, bald, rich and fat,
A buffalo. Women
Sniff. Men look away.
Drink liquor. Faces
Will appear, and tell you
Things you cannot bear."

       Pshaw. My Dad,
Dead since I was a kid, could hunker down
Across this campfire. I wouldn't turn
A hair. Gone, I will have all the time
Left in the world, so why regret
Someone I did or didn't kiss, a woman's
Curse, a bad review. Enough
To wear one saddle out on many mounts,
To keep a cool head on the edge
Of the Divide, new rivers spilling left
Or right, uncivilized, rugged, polite.
One thing scares me: done,
I'm just the parts I played. Stars
Fade. See, I traded hope, my share
In common happiness, to rise
Above the heads of men, to shine
For others passing on the prairie,

Sound and light enough to fill a dark
Room, quiet, strong, and true. A man
Of flesh and blood does not expect
To walk the earth forever. Shadows do.

AFTERWORD

Just because a man doesn't wear his heart on his sleeve, people think he has no inner life. But it takes more consideration to lead a life of action, than to be a man of words. Anyone who doubts the justice of this observation need look no farther than these poems, spoken over a great distance by a man of few words.

Besides the pleasure and excitement I knew attending his recitations, the Duke's visits provoked me to ponder any number of questions. Of course, I was more than a little intimidated by the star's presence. As reluctant to impede the incredible flow of verses from his tanned, translucent self, as I was certain that here was a spirit who would brook no cross-examination, several months passed before I felt confident enough to pose the obvious.

One evening, after he had recited 'The Needful' to me, I asked the Duke when he began writing poetry. Why did he write? and how it was that he chose me to deliver his poems to the world?

"I didn't choose you. You chose me."

While I wrestled with that, the Duke gave me the benefit of his unique perspective:

"I can't say I ever decided to sit down and write, but all the time I spent waiting for my scenes, I would think. Maybe musing's the word. I'd think about where I was, and what I was doing, what happened, and why. I'd lots of time, and the bigger I got, the lonelier I grew. So no one'd interrupt me.

"If John Ford was directing, he'd have an accordion player squeezing out tunes the whole time, off camera and sometimes on. 'Red River Valley.' So there'd be this mournful music, and maybe the Tetons hanging over Jackson Hole, or the sheer cliffs of Monument Valley.

"I'd look a bit, and think some more, take a rest between the looking and the thinking and the hearing. And these poems sprung up, like flowers after spring rain in the desert.

"See, one reason I was so strong was that my insides and my outsides were the same. But an actor saying written lines doesn't have the chance to show his insides as his own. They belong to the part, to the people looking at you. Any actor tries to be his inside self inside a part, well, he just isn't doing his job. You have to ripple like a lake does when the wind crosses it, and shakes up that picture of the cloud on the surface. And who can say what's swimming underneath?

"Understand, I'm talking to you now, man to man. I'm not telling you anything I don't know for sure, so I wouldn't bother asking me questions about religion if I were you, because you can't know what you don't believe, and maybe there aren't any answers that you'd want to hear. So just keep plugging, Pilgrim."

Which was all he had to say on that score, which was already more than I expected.

A LOOK AHEAD

A LOOK AHEAD

My daughter's cello teacher Barbara told me:
"Time was, there were so many people in my life
To telephone, to tell the small news to,
One day wasn't long enough to talk to all of them
And practice too. You always have to practice.

"Years and friends slip off so quietly
It hardly registers, until you want to share
A wedding, what a grandchild said—forget
The concert hall—and no one's left to ring up
Who wants to hear, not anyone at all."

Myself, I've written so much I cannot remember
What I said, or where the lines came from—
Those eavesdropped conversations between strangers
        dropped from sight—
That I believe life hangs upon forgetting.

WHAT HAPPENED TO SEYMOUR

"Two years ago September we spent Labor Day
With my brother in Fort Lauderdale.
Summer done, we came back in good time
For Eli to start school. He went
To first grade for two days, felt sick. I took him
To the doctor: tests, then chemotherapy,
The hospital. He never walked outside again.

"I have known many good things in my life
And had them taken from me.
This I can accept. Not one minute
Of those three years spent with Eli
Did I not know I was blessed. Never
Had life looked perfect in my sight
Before. I can accept being bereft.

"But I cannot accept that Eli never had
The chance to know those good things.
Five months tending him to death.
Six months of nothing, then a year
Of unemployment. I returned to school
And found work as a substitute.
Now I teach a third grade class in Harlem.

"It's hard to have to go in every day.
Tomorrow is our Christmas pageant.
I can't even think of disappointment.

It's just I've lived to see more
Than I wished to see.
I'm glad you called, but sorry
That I cannot tell another story."

ONE STRATEGY

Do you like to work
    outside? indoors?
    standing up or sitting down?
Would you rather use
    your hands? your head?
    your good looks? someone else's
Money to get on, ahead, away
    with murder, would you
    rather duck for cover
Even though it's never over?

By the end my wife's mother was
    A head, gray curls turned
    to the side, the pillow
Hardly dented, feet, and under-
    neath the sheets two
    white balloons, no visitors
Outside the common sunroom.
    She turned face up. She
    said: I'm very tired.
And expired.

    A pendulum
    in the United Nations
    atrium swings by earth's
Rotation. Life imitates life, sometimes
    I fill in the blanks with

  plots—the good man
Steals the best man's girl, the adoptive
  parents pregnant finally,
   the muttered prayer for luck—
Sometimes with blanks.

SIDEREAL

"Mythology tricks people into thinking
There was such a god as Jupiter
About whom they tell fables, how
He takes the human form or animal
To sleep with women and young boys.

"There are no silly little fairy-tale gods,
But vast concealed powers link everything
That lives and moves. Those powers
Are the planets and the stars. A thinker
Such as you or I can map their workings,

"All known history. Tell me the time
And place of someone's birth and I will plot
The planets' influence upon that life,
Which sweep like shadows of the clouds
Across a continent. Nothing is hidden

"From one who knows, who wants to look.
There is no blank unconconscious, only patterns
Turning underneath the changeling face,
The mechanism of a clock.
Beethoven said—(a man whose stars

"Were greater than Napoleon's,
Which meant he had to work alone
Inside his century, ahead of those
Much later yet unborn who
Understood him)—Beethoven said,

"'I do not need religion, for I hear
What God would say if he did not use words.'
I never make a personal decision, much less
Begin a portrait without asking questions
Of the stars. This painting of a lady:

"I worked seven months to get the fabric
In her dress train right. In Germany
Where I grew up, theologians talked
Much about the mistranslations
Found in Martin Luther's Bible

"And the delusions they have bred.
Although the words tell that
The poor own the earth, they mean
That earth is all they own. The rest
Falls to the rich and powerful.

"Unlike Napoleon—who marched
And millions followed—who fought to rule,
Not conquer, Hitler was not
Heaven's darling. Now I must tell the truth
About where Hitler came from:

"After World War I,
Four astrologers from Thule
Discovered someone had been born
At a rare marriage in the stars:
Through him coursed the origin

"Of German spirit. Like lamas
In Tibet, they sought the child
Described by this nativity,
And having found him, taught him
Who he was, and where his purpose lay.

"Alas, they were not alchemists also.
For Hitler, having learned his power
Turned against his teachers.
Neither creators nor their creature
Could transmute Hitler's baseness into gold.

"Those four wise men did not believe
Completely in the powers they uncovered:
They thought because they know they could
Control. And this is just as true today.
Astrology can lay out future history

"Precisely, this and other things which you
Might want to know. But few possess
The wisdom to see through those children's stories
Most men live by. Fewer want to hear
The answer, when they ask."

Q&A

1

Earth is the heaven of hell, and Eden
    Is the hell of heaven, not heaven's
Earth, the place where jealous
    God could keep his zoo.

    The weekend biker said:
"Think it's an accident our bodies have nine holes
    And that there are nine planets?
It's in the Bible. Check it out."

2

A heavenly voice was heard. It said:
    "There is nothing on the road.
There's nothing in the trees.
    There is nothing left to look at—

"So what are you looking at?
    Why are you looking?"

An angel sat on a log at the edge
    Where nothing starts
And watched the fireflies in the fog,
    The tiger lilies in the hedge.

SONG IS ANGELS' BREAD

In my thirties I stopped strumming
The guitar, and figured
Save for the odd scrap of poem,
Some solemn bars, I'd never sing again.

What a person won't say
Makes him stronger. I lived
My whole life outside
Settled ways, and grew

Into a monument by hanging on
To gifts. They're a comfort
On the edge of the high cliff
With darkness falling.

It doesn't call for brains or nerve
To kill time, nor an act of will.
Even after death,
Free-wheeling down the hill

Without a bottom, lead figure
In a stranger's dream,
The flickering has kept me here
Beyond my own remembering.

Any fool can love himself.
Better to be someone else's
Disappointment. I have no words
For somebody in love with nothing.

THE DEATH VINE

Propagates

As runner, torn

Up roots blood

Red, stem fat.

Tendrils

Wrap the host

Tree, mimic

The host leaves,

Choke the sap,

Light, life.

Flowerless,

Fruitless,

Lashed aloft,

Living on

Branches, even

With root cut,

Leaping through

Treetops, the vine

Is a squirrel,

A grackle,

A cockroach,

Sea urchin,

Mildew.

Spare hours,

I try to

Contain it.

SERIAL

One by one I gave up
Women, smoking, alcohol
And staying up past midnight.
Today, a calm, warm January Thursday
I pruned the sour cherry and dwarf apple trees.
The effort made me drunk
And, coming to, I heard first
Windchimes, then the backwash
Of cats in a great hurry. I lost my keys.

I'd much prefer to cash my check at leisure
After chatting with my broker, my foundation,
Over a shore dinner, but
Now past fifty I dance more to numbers,
Less to water-colored tunes of what might be.
"Give me lucre," Byron cried out to his publisher,
Arriving at the age lust feeds on money.

My mother has the flu. She's been inside for days
And cackles: "I look like the devil."
While Mitch, who's in good shape
And health complains his head's now round,
No longer suits his body: "Imagine
A thin man with Winston Churchill's head."

Sometimes walking past a mirror
I make the same mistake, and look, and wonder
Who that chilly, moon-faced man is,
No longer warm beside the devil's fire.

CARTOONIST!

The sky broke in, and said:
> "I'm sorry, but your time is up.
> I have to interrupt you now.
> If you continue talking I won't listen."

My wife broke in.
> "The sky said no such thing.
> How can you say such things?"

She may be right.
> The darkness of enlightenment.

Sit outside with the dogs, and watch the storm.

PACIFIC RIM

The souls peer down
    Through their canoe
At earth and air
    Floating below
"An evil day
    Has brought us here"
"I do not know
    Where else to go"

The turtle weeping
    Sisal tears
Will grow accustomed
    To its shell
A baby rides its
    Mother's thigh
Through wooden doors
    Through walls of stone

Our cockroach heads
    Between our knees
We dig long furrows
    With a will
Our father built
    That paled rim

For night to keep
> The salt stars in

These steady strokes draw
> Strength from him

ROMANTIC

ROMANTIC

Instead of growing into an old man
    I will become a dragon.
What does that mean exactly?
    Haven't got there yet. Don't know.
Just because the words are whispered
    In a single breath and quickly
Doesn't make them intimate.
    There's no inside out there, or here.

Get used to being wronged for life,
    Waiting to be turned into a sage
By one's own efforts! Without even trying!
    O rabbis of the bookish covens,
Do not give your tricks away for free.
    Do not give your tricks away.
I'm frightened by the ease of it:
    How our riches stole away
Before we ever knew we had them
    Snatched from our lips, unwanted kisses.

But now I know that which I did not
Want to know, and hardly feel I know it.

CONFEDERATE BREASTWORKS

At a novelty-antiques shop in Monterey, Virginia
(Highland County, the Switzerland of...)
The owner pointed to a silvered shard
And said: "Stonewall Jackson's shaving mirror."
— Or maybe it was J.E.B. Stuart's, or R.E. Lee's —
And didn't all those generals wear beards?
They wouldn't shave themselves?
For a history buff, that fugitive glimpse
Of whichever long-gone rebel leader
Looking at himself had left a trace
Between the silver backing and the glass—
As did my own, I guess, despite my spotty memory—
Which is the burden of this last reflection.

OPEN AND SHUDDER

Would you rather be a Spartan or Athenian?
Be free from want, or free to fail? Would you
Rather have a better-looking nose
Or hair, or tail? Dented by time's hammer
Strokes, a chained dog wails.

Time to stick a fork in the potatoes,
To read wisdom books with pleasure.
To wake up every morning with the thought
"That cold foot on my chest," and rolling
Out of bed not fear the wind growl
In the trees, the sun grown hard.

One Black Sea tribe dug holes beneath their dung hills,
And lived there. Nonetheless (Strabo reports)
They took uncommon interest in both art
And music. Make the world inside
You larger than the one around you
Or feel squeezed, like rats do when they breed
In cages. And no work without pay.

FABULOUS, BUT NOT ALOUD

When Amiri Baraka/ Leroi Jones
Was busted on a weapons charge
    In the 1960s, writers
Held a demonstration shouting:
    Lyres Speak the Truth.
Allen Ginsberg led the chanters;
The trial was in all the papers:
    Leroi Jones was jailed.

    In the 1980s,
New York Mayor Edward Koch (that rhymes
    With botch, not coke) promoting
One of his best-sellers, spoke
    At the New York PEN Club
About himself and politics
    And making war on drugs.

        Ginsberg,
Rising from the audience,
Asked the Mayor in one breath if he
"Supported the conspiracy
    between drug companies
And vampire landlord warlord lobbies
    that make ordinary
citizens criminals, criminals rich
    though government authority
    does not extend to ecstasy and

Mister Mayor will the prisoners
of conscience ever be set free?"

    Koch chanted down the poet:
"OM! Allen, OM! OM! OM! OM!"
    (Pronounced to rhyme with bomb, not comb.)
A humorist once told me: "I love poets,
    They are great to steal from."

WRITTEN ON THE DAY DEAD GHOSTS ARE FED

They came, flying down the red carpet,
Ate, paid their respects, and went home,
Each with a small bag of favors:
A bracelet, a mirror, a comb.
That night, the rare sound of rainfall.
Tomorrow, then New Moon, then Spring!

I'd like to stay and hear your dreams
But what you see is what it seems:
Today awakens in you, or you're taken.

A NOTE ON YEATS

According to Polybius
The sea route to Byzantium
Was fortunate in ways not clear
When looking at the map.
Across the Bosporus, Cyzicus
Seemed no less favored than its neighbor,
But its port was inaccessible
To boats sailing direct:
Voyagers from the Black Sea
Were swept by currents west and south
Into the harbor of Byzantium
Even when the wind held fair
For passage into Cyzicus.
A sailor from the south
Bound for Cyzicus from Greece
Or Syria was blown off-course
By the prevailing winds
Directly to Byzantium.
In those times, one could not
Not sail to Byzantium.

SABA'S NURSERY RHYME

You are the small cloud, I am the breeze
    I can push you wherever I please
Anywhere around the sky
    I won't give you any peace

Night time, you settle in back of the mountains
    Small cloud, and swallow a cavernous yawn
Nestle down, patter dreams wait while you crawl
    Under white covers blown by a squall

GUILTY, WITH AN EXPLANATION

"Six days his figure walked toward me
In the hall outside his room
His hair combed as he combed his hair
His glasses on, his arms spread wide
To greet me, and I knew
Although he could not leave the bed
I knew my father was still with us."

   —And on the seventh day?
"No more. I didn't see him move
Although his left side twitched as restlessly
As when his self lived there."

   —There is a trace of the true self
Accessible to love and knowledge
Invisible to the clinician's eye
Who could not bear to see such things
So many times upon the rounds
And never grasp its knees—I mean
The soul outlives expression
And calls forth recognition
Until it's time to go.

LONG AND SHORT

Mitch said: "I'm trying hard to live
    To seventy."
I think about it constantly:
    How half
A century is an abyss not all
    Can cross—
"This field, once, was home to brains
    And tigers—"
And paint the mystery, how time
    (A wheel)
Describes the line (that's history)
    On earth
Where people (at the tangent point)
    Buckle,
Bear the weight, or run behind,
    Or break
Into those dances oceans sing
    To dunes,
Or ice.
    Leon Schapiro fled
        The terror
First to Paris then New York.
    A chronicler
Of the Jews, white hair, blue eyes,
    Wood cane,

Beret, right off he said: "We need
    A lawyer.
To be old is terrible."
    Howard,
Eighty, in Jamaica, kept
    Two wives,
A shop and the beach towel concession.
    Ninety,
Jimmy asked his son's wife's friend
    To come
Away with him, to fish in warmer seas.
    The landlord,
Heller, rhymed behind his desk:
    "Money's honey.
How does that help
    When you're old
        And it's cold
            In your soul?
My son is so religious he
    Won't eat
At the same table with me."
    Once
I didn't hear at all, or hearing
    Thought
The softly said need not
    Be marked,

And turned back to the book,
    The board,
The ball beneath the sycamore.
    My father
Also thundered like the god
    Who's killed
Most, doesn't wonder about might
    Have been.
"Have you changed at all
    In order
To live longer?" "No, as always
    Exercise,
Right food and rest. Also avoid
    The doctor."
Also disbelieve in numbers.

TODAY
So much rain
The air between
The trees is green,
As is the gray.

GLIB CONFUCIAN, GARRULOUS LLULLIST

I have felt it in my heart
I have done it in my pants
I have thought it through in daylight
I have asked it to a dance
I've committed it in writing
I have grasped it in the dark
I have gone without companions
Through the ramble, in the park
I have shown it in a movie
And denied it to my face
Made an altar of the mirror
Taken pride in my disgrace
I have touched it up in photos
I have taken it on tour
I've walked it twice around the block
To help it feel secure
I have told my dreams about it
To near strangers in the street
I have stroked it under covers
I have fed it to the cat
I have smothered it with curses
And inflated it with smacks
I've done everything but name it
As it slithers through the cracks

I could go on forever
But I don't believe I will
Though it occupies the emptiness
And does expand to fill

A SOMETIME THING

Reading Kenneth's salad poems
      From 50 years ago,
From 50 years ago when I was seven:
    There is no greater luxury
Or freedom that the mind can know, although
    About the soul I can't be certain:
Open the curtains so the day flows through: air and light
    And comets blowing trumpets.
Kisses would be kinder to the ear, but slight.

THE LAST PART OF LONGING

Rabbi Judah and Rabbi Jose were walking.
Jose remembered how his father told him
Years before that, in the very place
They had just left, in his sixtieth year
Jose would find a treasure. "I now am sixty,"
Jose said, "but have not found the treasure.
Could it be the words we have just spoken
Are the treasure that my father meant?"
Rabbi Judah stopped and could not answer.

Jose turned aside into a cave.
In the dark, between two rocks, he found
A book, which he brought out into the light.
Opening the book, Jose saw
Rubbings of the seventy-two letters
Given Adam, by which means he knew
All the higher and the lower wisdom,
All that would occur up to the end
Of time. As the scholars ventured deeper
Into Adam's aleph-beth, a fire
Wind plucked the book out of their hands.

The two walked on to Simeon bar Yohai,
And told him of the wisdom they discovered.
"Perhaps you were looking at those letters
That tell when the Messiah's time will come?"
He asked. They could not answer Simeon,

Because they had forgotten all they'd read.
"Ah," said the Kabbalist. "The Holy One
Does not permit these things to be revealed
Now, but when the time is near at hand
Nothing will be hidden. Little children
Will sport with wisdom yet undreamed by us,
And tell true stories of the world to come."

AIR ON THE SIDE OF PRUDENCE

I think that I am suffering
From post-neurotic stress disorder:
A random thought? an ordered world? or either other?

Seated at the table with Oedipus and Isaac,
The conversation turned to parenting:
"I wish I'd kept a journal when I had a life."
"I seized the lisping ethnarch by his yard of beard…"

Another voice, less cosmic, said:
"Three robins are embroidering the borders with fat worms."
How did I turn out so severe?

So Chinese, Chaucer, Krazy Kat and Moses?
And can make nothing of it?
In fancy not in fact I killed my father
And figured where he ends, there I begin.

Like snowfall on the grown bamboo
I have no roots, just baggage.
No words for god, but talk's religion, leading…

Leading? leading where?
I met a woman at a concert
Whose husband of twelve years
Left her for the sister of their best-friend-couple's wife,

Who then dated her next-door neighbor,
Who went on a charity bicycle tour to Savannah
Where he joined a group called "The Twelve Tribes."

He said she could marry the tribe with him
But she'd have to give up her dogs;
And two trees fell on her home last Sunday.
And the power is still out.

I think that with the best will in the world
We drive our long-time friends away,
Who may not go, but do not want to stay.

OPUS POSTHUMOUS

The cast bronze bust of Sigmund Freud
Beside my father's desk lamp said:
"Practice, and believe me this is all
The afterlife you can look forward to—"
    A talking head upon a table-top.

My ignorance still gives me room to hope,
To conjure up the egg with legs,
The Jew who says, "Says who?"
That me? "Who died from complications
    Of a fall." Don't we all?

SMALL EMOTIONS ARE THE CAPTAINS OF OUR LIVES

1

When my father's death was reported
By the New York Psychoanalytic Society
A quarter-century ago, he called me up:
"Please inform my colleagues that it is not so."
I telephoned the newsletter editor,
Co-author of their book on drug addiction,
Who listened and responded, "Are you sure?"

2

An eerily warm March day 2010,
I waited for my sometime Doppelgänger
On a bench in Verdi Square (once Needle Park)
For fifteen minutes past the time appointed.
So well I know myself, I tried to reach him
By mobile first, then rang at home.
A hit. "Have I made some mistake?
Is this today? You're sure it's not tomorrow?"

3

One sunny day, I read *The Art of War* and made
A list of opposites like self and other,
Live long live well, the Pope and Luther,
Users, lovers, a cosmic how-to book of leanings
And stared into the mirror: have my ears grown
Longer? shorter? does the hair create illusion?
The old Taoist kept a tortoise in his bathtub
And rode the elevator hoping he would meet
Young girls: the secrets of longevity.

HARP

I looked to the prairie
Gray rain hung in curtains
The west wind made ripples
Across hip-high grass
I thought of the old friends
The good ones, the bad ones
Who'd gone west before me
And emptied my glass

It's better to have hair
Like snow than be falling
Like leaves from an aspen
Like stars in July
The campfire's cold but
An autumn night's colder
Than charge account kisses
Returned on the sly

I never believed that
Love lasted forever
Or the Snake River never
Spilled into the sea
I took my sweet time
Driving shadows to market
And never remarked at
The herd driving me

Don't cry in the morning
Don't talk if you're leaving
Don't ask how the change
Overtakes us some day,
How fire when you touch
Soon feels colder than starlight
At night in the desert:
That I couldn't say

COMMON ANCESTOR

COMMON ANCESTOR

For forty years I started every day from scratch.
For forty years I lived each day as though it were the last.

Now I have no idea how many days remain, or years
But want to live them out without regret, or bitterness.

The old men have retreated to their games
Of golf, of chess, of second-guessing.

The younger ones don't feel any kinship,
Eyes sharp for the leg up and happy chance.

I soldier on alone, though I've grown better
Both at learning and explaining what I know.

I miss my part in other people's worlds,
Don't recognize the language floating out their doors.

Which would you rather lose, your mind or body?
Fool's paradise? Who cares who owns it, just so it is there.

WISDOM OF THE GATED COMMUNITY

We bought a new lamp shade,
    four storage containers,
a printer and scanner
    and raked up the leaves:
A week of achievement:
    No weaponized worry,
bare trees, citrus moonrise:
    A camera-shy madman.

Wash hands after rising, and then
    wash your eyes.
I read to be steadied
    with no claim to wisdom.
I won't say that book's name
    but splash in the aftersound,
my white hairs grown dark again.
    The ocean turned shallow.

Now late, Ellen entered
    my sleep in a red dress.
Wide-shouldered, she stood
    on the city street pointing
across at a brownstone stoop:
    "I didn't move here
to watch my best friend die." Soul
    flung like a stone from a sling.

A cannister vacuum hose
    draped round my neck,
I'm the man in the moon
    without lantern, or thorn bush,
or old dog, or ash bin.
    This book has no pictures.
And waggles its long beard.
    That dream tore my pillow.

ORGANIZED DESOLATION

I want to be a throwaway
I want to be a mass-market item
I want to be a fund-raising promotion
I want to be
    History
Here and gone before you know it
A value-added package of vicarious excitement
Just a blip off the radar, star of eternity
On a mountain of money, I want to be
    History

END OF THE MIDDLE CLASS LINE

I woke up with my eyes ablaze,
A demon from the Japanese,
But it was only allergies
And terror of the mirror.

My mother's neighbor beckoned her:
Come see my new refrigerator.
My mother said: a nurse, a purse
Is all the old ones look for.

Like Socrates said in his cups
To anyone who'd listen: Whoops!
What is the difference between
Being and pretending?

Don't answer that. A wise king kills
His enemies with kindness, pills.
I cramped the full moon in my head
And made my living father dead.

Some day I'll visit Portugal,
Its seaports, where Pessoa wrote
"You can be happy in Australia,
As long as you don't go there."

The redbird in the redbud sang
A two-note song, on March's bough:
The primal scene's our parents talking:
Unbearable, like angels singing.

In truth, most truth is doggerel
The soul walks on a schedule.
So who will clean up after me,
Or mop brown sauce with money?

To those who said, "You will be dead
Before you're understood," I say:
The flies were very slow last May.
I mean to make you wait.

"WE LOVE THESE MACHINES LIKE WE LOVE OUR OWN CHILDREN"

If you knew you would never
Speak to someone later should you
Talk more to that person now, or not?

If you could talk once more
One last time to someone gone
Forever, would you? Could you not?

How far would you go
Just to have a cup of coffee?
What would you ask? What say?

Wish at once for rain
And sun? Want to be certain
Everything that can be said is done?

ORIENTALIA

Moon and stars and scimitars,
    A piece not in its place—
Those things a scholar clings to—
    Deliver me from solemnity:

Otherwise I turn into a pretzel
    Trying to seem natural,
Listening for birdcalls
    In a marathon leaf fall.

"ONE" IS THE LIGHT THAT SHINES BY DAY

I saw my mother in three dream tableaux:
The first, she was a younger woman, clothed;
The second, she was seated, nude, and posed
So only her profile, back, and upraised arm
    As if to shield, showed;
Third, there was an empty ottoman,
    And an abandoned robe.

    My mother said:
"If you don't look into the mirror,
    How will you recognize
        The one you are?"
(As distinguished from the one I think I am?)

Who has invented something out of nothing?
    Spring days are hung on ladder rungs,
        And drying.
What once was tasted through the eyes,
    Then later with the mouth,
        By nature,
Now must be done by cunning.

FOUR OLD GERMAN LOVE SONGS

1

    Green trees bud all around.
    Will my young man come round?
    Has he mounted and ridden away?
With whom will my fingers, toes, lips, teeth, tongue play?

2

    Where it comes, there it goes
    The young women are chasing
    All this hot summer long
    That one thing they are missing.

3

    If the world were all mine
    From the Alps to the Rhine's
    Mouth I'd give it away
    So that she, in my dream
    Woke, her hand on my thigh.

4

    A little bird sang in the woods
    To the dust red rose late in September:
    The heartbeat, the heart beats forever?
    We have this one night, which grows longer.

RABBINIC HYMN

All that lives by breathing makes a blessing of your name,
Lord, and the spirit makes its praise when it remembers
How it was from the beginning to the end that without God
There is no way to save ourselves, no freedom, no providing
Against the time of trouble, no good feeling. Only one
Who made the universe and sees time in one glance
Deserves our songs, our praise. No nod, no blink, no dream
But God in the material jolts us, wakes us, gives us speech
That breaks our bondage, steadies wavers, sets us straight.

Praise only one. If our mouths held sounds like oceans water
And our tongues rippled standing waves, our lips stretched wide
As the horizon, our eyes both sun and moon, our hands spread
Wings like eagles on the updraft, our feet light,
It were not enough to thank you, praise you, say your name
Which can't be said, for all done for our fathers and for us.

You brought us out of Egypt and the house of bondage,
Fed us in famine, let us prosper amid plenty,
Saved us from the sword, the plague, from evil and disease.
As you have helped us until now, may you always
Keep us, God, upon the side of mercy.

And so we raise our arms, and dance, and sing, and speak
(Your gifts) inspired by the need to name,
Each mouth a thanks, each tongue an oath, each knee
Bent, thumping on the hollow earth as we remember
All that lives by breathing makes a blessing of your name.

SALADIN

That so much love and wrath should pass through me
And nothing left but stories, sand and stars:

These enemies who see their own worst selves
In us, weak tribes who hate each other so

That only by remembering Jerusalem
Was ours before and after it was theirs,

Before and after Esau, Abraham and David,
Can we see past ourselves and follow me.

Because we have no home except our bodies,
Because they are no nation but a book,

I raise my arm and point to the old city.
It would be shameful to command this people

And die with one day's maintenance in hand,
Returned to dust yet leave a lump behind.

UNDERSTOOD

She said: If only I could find the songbird's perch
    By ear, if eyes could follow sound.
I said: They can. Look: that gray catbird
    In the redbud turns the color of the leaves.
She: I see. But look away and, even if the bird remains,
    The sight if not its song is lost.
Like reading from a Torah scroll:
    Look up for just a moment and
You lose the place, and must fall silent
    Until you find your place again.

PEREK SHIRAH: A CHAPTER OF SONG

The *Perek Shirah*, an ancient Hebrew poem of indeterminate origin, places a biblical or rabbinic passage in the mouth of each of the eighty-four parts of creation as recounted in Genesis, from Heaven to dogs.

Some commentaries say King David wrote the poem. In the tenth through the sixteenth century, Ashkenazic and Sephardic versions served as a portable liturgy. One tradition states in the name of Yehudah the Prince that immersion in the *Perek Shirah* delivers the student from the Evil Impulse, and prolongs life. If this were not enough, Rabbi Eliezer the Great promises: "Anyone who recites even part of 'A Chapter of Song' in this world, sings it with Moses in the world to come."

The Sages said that
> David, when his Psalms were done

Grew proud, and looking at the sky, said:
> What in all Creation's
> Sung more songs than I?

A bullfrog happened by. He said:
> David, don't be so puffed-up.
> At dusk I croak ten times more songs,
> More praises than you twanged in your whole life.
> > More,
>
> Each twang of mine sounds like 3,000 meanings,
> > Every one a blessing.
>
> You feed the heron wading in still water?
> Do you hear what you can see?
> Then help me finish singing:

ONE

Heaven says:

> To see clearly's sweet as sunlight
> On an autumn shoulder, shining on the face
> Of harder laws than stone.

And Earth:

> No where is empty.
> Any door lets angels
> Go and come. Hear
> Wingbeats past an open window.

Eden says:

> Open your eyes.
> It won't make you happy.
> It might make you wise.

The Abyss says:

> Prisoners of self, of taste, they found
> No food to like, and did not eat, and would have died.

The Desert:

> Promise blossoms to the thirsty.
> Flint can pierce a heart past longing.

Fields say:

> The land has reasons of its own;
> It flaunts the night sky's understanding.

Lakes say:
> Lightning kisses the water.
> Mists rise from the shoreline.
> Wind baffles rolled thunder.

Oceans sound:
> Waves: the deep's pulse, a heartbeat.

Rivers run:
> Mouths open into the ocean.

Wellsprings say:
> Being, the known song of dancers.

TWO

The Day says:
> Day speaks to day;
> Night tells night what it knows.

Night observes:
> Morning's kind. See,
> It follows me constantly.

Sun says:
> My home is the center.
> The moon turns around you.
> My beams are the axle.

The Moon answers:
> Festivals keep time by moon phase, but
> Only the sun knows when darkness will come.

Stars whisper:
> Count on us. Sight beggars numbers,
> Swarms of light stung into being.

Storm Clouds say:
> Darkly, our heads sway like sea grass
> Riding deep currents,
> Gusts from the seabed.

Thin Clouds whistle:
> Breeze, scatter sunlight like seeds.

The Wind shouts:
> North and south, listen up:
> Bring your daughters and sons
> From the ends of the earth.
> Know where that begins?

Lightning:
> Whose kiss turns water to vapor?
> Who packs the winds' bags in trunks made of cloud?

Dew says:
> O rose bush, o cedar, o hedge,
> Garden and orchard nod
> North as the south wind blows.
> At sunrise, fruits blush.

The Rains say:
> Wash dust from the wasteland and heartland.

THREE

The Forest says:
> Trees sing the chorus
> When no one can hear it.

Vines jingle:
> In clusters
> We press grapes upon you.

The Fig says:
> Suck honey.
> Who gives shall be given.

Pomegranate:
> In rows like bright teeth,
> My seeds stain your lips.
> You answer:
> With pleasure.

Palms:
> Clap, taller
> Than cedars on tiptoe
> On mountains,
> I cast a long shadow,
> Am seen from afar.

The Citron says:
> Eve knew my wood
> Was good for food,
> As is my fruit.

Wheat:
> In Eden my stalks grew like trees.
> Here silos are laden.

Barley says:
> Barely crumbs,
> Riches for paupers.

Weeds:
> Meadow-grazed flocks leap
> Flat rocks barked with lichens,
> Hillsides and roadsides
> Ravished by green.

Vegetables:
> In the damp, in the dark, in long furrows
> On earth we await both your hand and your mouth.
> Even here.

Grasses:
> Each herb has its own star
> Which forces new growth.
> Lost with us?
> Last with us.

FOUR

The Rooster says:

> The Maker hears trees blowing
>
> Spices in Eden and, scenting their praise,
>
> Arises and sings aloud: So,

At first light roosters crow:

> Roll up your clanging gates! Open your doors!

Second call:

> Lift your head! Sunlight knocks!

Third chorus:

> Get up! Won't tell you who's coming!

Fourth he clangs:

> Sound alarm! Daytime brews!

And fifth calls out:

> Dolt! Sluggard! Deadbeat! Bolt upright!

The sixth call's persuasion:

> Who loves sleep
>
> Loves only himself!
>
> Open eyes! Open eyes!

The seventh:

> Act now! There are limits!

The Hen says:

> Here's food for the living.

Doves burble:
> Better bitter food, olives
> Plucked from the open land
> Than honeyed grain tendered
> By some human master.
> I coo, I soar.

Vultures say:
> Serve my meat at the roadside.

Cranes cry:
> Sing me grace, for my neck is a harp.

The Songbird chirps:
> In a hedge, in the ivy, in thorns
> Build the sparrow's nest, safe for the hatch.

Swallows:
> Under eaves, in the loft,
> If you please, if you please.

Swifts twitter:
> Rise in puffs from the chimneys,
> In flocks on the wing.

Storm Petrels:
> See earth below clouds,
> Oceans studded with green islands,
> Capped and footed by iced poles.

The Bat pings:
> Comfort in the dark.

The Stork:
> I speak kindness.
> Whole cities are pardoned.

Raven croaks:
> The world is my banquet.

Starlings:
> Land in a blanket, a black cloud, an ink blot.

Tame Geese say:
> This barnyard was given to us
> When there were just a few of us,
> So we know where we come from.

The Wild Goose cries:
> Make way! Make way!
> We are vees in the sky,
> And find food in the waste, on the flyway.

Ducks:
> Stale bread by the pond,
> Grass and worms from the mud.

The Bee-Eater's song:
> In sunshine, in jungles
> I snatch buzzers in flight,
> A bird's mead.

Grasshoppers speak:
>   You are to me, as I am
>   In the eyes of the high ones;
>   Trapped in a jar,
>   I jump upward, and fall.

The Locust prates:
>   Flex my nose.
>   I eat green shoots.
>   I have no king.

The Spider opens:
>   My web is a curtain the small cannot see,
>   And the great cannot see through.

The Fly opines:
>   What table is not set for me?
>   And all are my enemy.
>   In this place, such is peace.

Sea Monsters say:
>   We make lions of our own device,
>   But not alone.
>   We play short rags in dragon deeps.

Leviathan:
>   Shouldering waves,
>   I spout, and dive.
>   Cold oceans hum along.

Fish schoolwork:
> Wind draws longhand script on open water.
> That voice is there, the thunder's and the waters'.

The Frog's short speech:
> Born under water, I breathe air.
> A riddle, David? Maybe more?

FIVE

Flocks baa:

>By the Red Sea, none beside you, none like you.

Cows low:

>Jerusalem.
>
>Cows are too lingual.
>
>Beware the black bull.

Pigs grunt:

>We're chosen by heart, not by lot.

Beasts of Burden say:

>Labor flavors our fodder.

The Camel:

>Who trudges below, hears the wind roar in dry skies,
>
>Watches dunes walk, remembers fresh water.

Horse neighs:

>Via hands, heels and clucks master talks.
>
>I think but one thought, one thought at a time.
>
>And sleep on my feet.

The Mule:

>This harsh voice be born from my mother, the jenny;
>
>The dam of a shrill-voiced mule is a mare.
>
>White mules kick and kill.

Donkeys bray:
> Even the slave in charge of the water pits,
> Thanks to his work, enters heaven.

The Ox:
> Mute, recites in another's voice, inwardly:
> The horse and its rider thrown into the sea.

Wild Beasts say:
> One day will see a covenant for us,
> And we will keep it.

Gazelles say:
> I sleep one eye open.
> My name is a love song.

The Elephant trumpets:
> Who made great strange creatures
> Made you: Hear, remember, and do.

The Lion:
> My roar, like that bitter herb fed to the captive,
> Inarticulate power.

The Bear says:
> On mountains, by rivers, in forest and cities,
> Pursue them!

Wolves:
> Every human offense takes the name of an animal.
> This is it: like your innocence, howling and lurking.

The Fox yips:
> Were I a man, I would not act like a fox.

Hounds bay:
> Come! Follow! Come follow!

The Cat spits:
> Climb the high rafters and nest by the roof beam,
> I will scratch you down.

The Mouse sniffs:
> I am small, but the enemy still has not caught me.

Cat growls:
> Got you now, in my paws, as my plaything.

Mouse allows:
> There's some justice in that.

SIX

Insect Swarms:

> Gnats rise and fall in the light,
> Cams in a transparent engine.

Creeping Things:

> Those with tongues speak through the mouth;
> Those without speak through their numbers.

The Snake says:

> What use hissing evil?
> Ask the whisperer set on deception.
> My tongue flicks at psalms in the dust.
> Such is my mission.

The Scorpion says:

> Every sting has its remedy:
> For the wasp, steep bark of date-palm in water;
> For me, mix the gall of a white stork in beer.

The Snail:

> Today, maybe one on a mountain.
> Tomorrow, when rain falls: a mountain of snails.

Ants say:

> A shadow has fallen.
> We have no king, and gather all summer.

The Rat:

> Only the dead do not fear me.

Dogs say:
> Bow down. Or not.
> Like the cock among fowls, like the dog among beasts,
> So the chosen among nations.

~

A young man fasted eighty-five times, objecting:
> Dogs eat dung. They get to sing?

An angel answered:
> Eat.
> No dog bared fangs at Moses
>> When he led you out of Egypt.
> Dog dung tans the hides
>> Our scrolls are written on.
> Dogs earned their song.
> You, watch your tongue.

INDEX OF TITLES AND FIRST LINES

A bow tie, a green bow tie with sparkles: 141
A leaf, when torn, becomes 102
A little man might have to get 161
A LOOK AHEAD 181
A man may earn millions, ... 136
A NOTE ON YEATS 207
A shadow box where Pierrot 74
A SOMETIME THING 216
A stone bench in the cotton shadows. 137
According to Polybius 207
AFFECT 46
AFTERWORD 176
AIR ON THE SIDE OF PRUDENCE 219
All that lives by breathing makes a blessing of your name, ... 237
An almost real speculation—parts 84
An easy way to take off weight, ... 171
ANATOMY 75
Any man who'd burn his draft card 149
ART HISTORY 107
At a novelty-antiques shop in Monterey, Virginia 202
At first, the sky included the earth. 24
At sunset, the campers take 103

BEGIN. THE LIGHT IS HONEY. 17
BIG MEDICINE 165
BLACK ELK SPEAKS 143
BLACK HAT, WHITE HAT 173
Body is to spirit 98
BORDERLAND 160
BROWN CATS IN THE DOG DAYS 57
BUFFALO GALS 152
Byron reborn as a suburban Jew, ... 83

CALIFORNIA	104
CARTOONIST!	196
CHORUS	52
CLOUDS	34
COMMON ANCESTOR	227
CONFEDERATE BREASTWORKS	202
CREDULOUS, ALL GOLD	84
CRUSADE SONG	64
CURRICULUM VITAE (1978)	83
Days are skirts, and years the wind that raises them.	79
DEAR ABBY	80
Dear Abby:	80
Dinosaurs died with meat on their bones	142
Do not begin far from us	52
Do you like to work	184
Don't think back much	168
DOUBT SERENE	72
DOWNSTAIRS ON THE GLOBE	131
DUKE: THE POEMS	147
Earth is the heaven of hell, and Eden	190
"Economics, Andrea, my love	93
EMBLEM	74
END OF THE MIDDLE CLASS LINE	231
Eve stepped from the doorway	17
FABULOUS, BUT NOT ALOUD	204
FAME	142
FINISH UP	102
FLAGSTONE	112
For forty years I started every day from scratch.	227
FOUR OLD GERMAN LOVE SONGS	236
FOXGLOVE, SOURCE OF DIGITALIS	105
From time to time all	22

GARDEN INTELLIGENCE	137
GERTRUDE AND SAMUEL	29
Get up at ten o'clock, eat a little breakfast,	33
GLIB CONFUCIAN, GARRULOUS LLULLIST	214
GNOSIS IN PRAGUE	82
God is so angry with us	114
"GOD, SIR." THEN SHE WAS QUIET	78
GOOFY IN THE MIDDLE	132
GOOFY'S BRUSH WITH DESPAIR	134
GRAUMAN'S CHINESE	164
Green trees bud all around.	236
GUILTY, WITH AN EXPLANATION	209
HAPPINESS IS MY BEAT	118
HARD TO BELIEVE	163
HARP	223
HASTENING THUS	35
Hello there, little lady.	152
HELLO, PILGRIM	161
Here where the jetstreams rise,	39
HYMN	23
HYMN TO CREATION	47
"I am remember the time, in Italy	62
I ATE A MUFFIN AND IT WAS ENOUGH	53
I didn't want to act the goof	153
I have felt it in my heart	214
"I know an old woman	105
I looked to the prairie	223
I read a story yesterday:	57
I said to the psychiatrist:	107
I saw my mother in three dream tableaux:	235
I think that I am suffering	219
I want to be a throwaway	230
I went out and bought myself	134
I woke up with my eyes ablaze,	231

If you knew you would never	233
In 1954, in June	21
In my thirties I stopped strumming	191
INFATUATION	139
Instead of growing into an old man	201
IS THAT ALL?	116
"It is refulgent," said Rabbi Simeon, "this child,	46
"It must have been exciting,	69
It's lonely off the reservation,	170
Jeremy Bentham, Fichte and God	47
JULIA BLOOMFIELD: 24 JUNE 1974	79
Just because a man doesn't wear his heart	176
Just thinking about being	139
KACHINA	156
KING JAMES REGGAE	110
Like your psychology, my physics	51
LONG AND SHORT	210
Love answers	78
Marlene didn't like it when I rode	173
MASS CONFUSIONS AND ENTHUSIASMS	51
Mild but wild, April day with winds	121
Mitch said: "I'm trying hard to live	210
Moon and stars and scimitars,	234
My daughter's cello teacher Barbara told me:	181
My head aches, my right arm twinges, my stomach	118
My music was the crack	166
"Mythology tricks people into thinking	186
NO HARM DONE	55
Not yet and still was English spoken.	29

One afternoon in the lounge of the Gem Institute 104
One by one I gave up 194
ONE STRATEGY 184
"ONE" IS THE LIGHT THAT SHINES BY DAY 235
OPEN AND SHUDDER 203
OPUS POSTHUMOUS 221
ORGANIZED DESOLATION 230
ORIENTALIA 234
OVERLAND STAGE 168

PACIFIC RIM 197
PEREK SHIRAH: A CHAPTER OF SONG 241
PILLOW BOOK 121
POET, PICK UP THAT GUITAR 108
Propagates 193
PROPHYLAXIS 69
PUNCH AND JUDAISM 122

Q&A 190

Rabbi Judah and Rabbi Jose were walking. 217
RABBINIC HYMN 237
Reading Kenneth's salad poems 216
ROMANTIC 201

SABA'S NURSERY RHYME 208
SALADIN 238
SERIAL 194
She said: If only I could find the songbird's perch 239
SHOT DOWN 153
Sid, there are no words 164
SIDEREAL 186
"Six days his figure walked toward me 209
"Six month ago I was a rich man 116
SMALL EMOTIONS ARE THE CAPTAINS OF OUR LIVES 222

SO HIGH, SO LOW	62
So much rain	213
SOME HORSES AND SOME COWS	141
Someone wants mercy for himself alone	41
SONG (FROM THE TAMIL)	136
SONG IS ANGELS' BREAD	191
SOUNDTRACK	166
Spend over half a century	157
Sunrise in the High Sierra,	154
SWISS INDEPENDENCE DAY	103
TARA	154
That so much love and wrath should pass through me	238
The author of The Incoherence of the Incoherence	72
The cast bronze bust of Sigmund Freud	221
THE CLASSICS	157
THE DEATH VINE	193
THE END OF AUTUMN	22
THE EXCHANGE	24
The first fall day	56
THE GIANT SUN'S SONG	67
THE GOOD LIFE	33
The hidden grows. Those chants and steps,	156
THE LAST CENTURY	56
The last day of July: the sun is out	55
THE LAST PART OF LONGING	217
THE LETTER "C"	171
The little tennis ball and the handball blown with wind	34
THE MAP OF JAPAN	99
The mixed multitude kills time in Kingston airport.	110
The moon waxed fat	129
THE NEEDFUL	170
The only state I've never been in is Alaska.	143
The painter took a slice of air	82
The parrot Mephistopheles learned to call the cat	60
The phone rang late last night:	132

THE ROOF	39
The Sages said that	243
THE SEARCHER	149
The sky broke in, and said:	196
The souls peer down	197
THE WANDERER	41
The world of the wind is woven warp and woof	23
Their faces weather in the picnic air.	32
Then love introduces the expensive dream	25
THESE ANEMONES, THEIR SONG	21
These feats of earth shall bring us to the air.	64
They came, flying down the red carpet,	206
THIS IS GOD	68
This is God as an ageing Jewish man.	68
This morning waiting for my ears to clear	53
This poor excuse for a singing cowboy	165
THREE GENERATIONS AT ONE TABLE ON THE PATIO	32
Three weeks of cold	131
To the south, a cloudburst	160
TODAY	213
TWO PRESENTS	60
"Two years ago September we spent Labor Day	182
UNDERSTOOD	239
VIA SATELLITE	129
Waking up each morning	163
Walking past an iris	112
WATER IS THE MOTHER OF ICE	25
We bought a new lamp shade,	228
"WE LOVE THESE MACHINES LIKE WE LOVE OUR OWN CHILDREN"	233
"We're just a couple nearly forty	99
WEALTH OF NATIONS	93
WHAT HAPPENED TO SEYMOUR	182

267

When Amiri Baraka/ Leroi Jones 204
When I was ten my family went to Europe, ... 35
When my father's death was reported 222
Who turned over in light 67
WISDOM OF THE GATED COMMUNITY 228
Would you rather be a Spartan or Athenian? 203
WRITTEN ON THE DAY DEAD GHOSTS ARE FED 206

Years pass like days, days 122
You are the small cloud, I am the breeze 208
"'You talk in rhyme, it always sounds 75
YOUR MELODIES 114

A NOTE ON THE COVER

Jonicus, fourth son of Noah, was born in the third year of the Flood; but as to him, Moses is silent. Jonicus first discovered the science of astronomy, and he prophesied future events.

—Hartmann Schedel, *Nuremberg Chronicle*, 1493

BOOKS BY LAURANCE WIEDER

POETRY

The Coronet of Tours
No Harm Done
Duke: The Poems as told to Laurance Wieder
The Last Century: Selected Poems
Ten Torch Songs
Words to God's Music: A New Book of Psalms
Perek Shirah: A Chapter of Song
PoemSite: Songs in the Landscape
After Adam: The Books of Moses
Isaiah's Closing Arguments: A New Translation

PROSE

Man's Best Friend: Photographs by William Wegman
Full Circle: Panoramas of Paris, Venice, Rome, Siena and Kyoto by Kenneth Snelson
Poetry History Music Art: Essays 1996-2017

ANTHOLOGIES

Chapters into Verse: Poetry in English Inspired by the Bible, Volume 1: Genesis—Malachi; Volume 2: Gospels—Revelation
King Solomon's Garden: Poetry and Art Inspired by the Old Testament
The Red Sea Haggadah
The Poets' Book of Psalms
Chapters into Verse: A Selection of Poetry in English Inspired by the Bible from Genesis through Revelation

www.ingramcontent.com/pod-product-compliance
Lightning Source LLC
Chambersburg PA
CBHW031101080526
44587CB00011B/769